Showing & TELLING

Learn How to Show & When to Tell
for Powerful & Balanced Writing

Laurie Alberts

WD
WRITER'S DIGEST
BOOKS
WritersDigest.com
Cincinnati, Ohio

For more resources for writers, visit www.writersdigest.com/books.

To receive a free weekly e-mail newsletter delivering tips and updates about writing and about Writer's Digest products, register directly at http://newsletters.fwpublications.com.

14 13 12 11 10   5 4 3 2 1

Distributed in Canada by Fraser Direct
100 Armstrong Avenue
Georgetown, Ontario, Canada L7G 5S4
Tel: (905) 877-4411

Distributed in the U.K. and Europe by David & Charles
Brunel House, Newton Abbot, Devon, TQ12 4PU, England
Tel: (+44) 1626-323200, Fax: (+44) 1626-323319
E-mail: postmaster@davidandcharles.co.uk

Distributed in Australia by Capricorn Link
P.O. Box 704, Windsor, NSW 2756 Australia
Tel: (02) 4577-3555

Library of Congress Cataloging-in-Publication Data
Alberts, Laurie.
Showing & telling : learn how to show & when to tell for powerful & balanced writing / by Laurie Alberts.
        p. cm.
Includes bibliographical references and index.
  ISBN 978-1-58297-705-8 (alk. paper)
  1. Creative writing--Handbooks, manuals, etc. 2. Authorship--Handbooks, manuals, etc. 3. English language--Rhetoric--Handbooks, manuals, etc. I. Title. II. Title: Showing and telling.
  PE1408.A447 2010
  808.3--dc22   2009051026

Edited by Scott Francis
Designed by Terri Woesner
Production coordinated by Mark Griffin

Dedication

To all my students past and present

About the Author

Laurie Alberts is the author of six books including three novels: *The Price of Land in Shelby*, *Lost Daughters*, and *Tempting Fate*. Her work has won several awards, including a James Michener Award. She teaches fiction and creative nonfiction in the MFA in Writing Program at Vermont College of Fine Arts. Her website is www.lauriealberts.com.

Table OF CONTENTS

Section One
Making Vibrant Scenes

Section Two
Creating Essential Summaries

Section Three
Combining Scene and Summary

Introduction

Inexperienced fiction and creative nonfiction writers are often told to show, not tell—to write scenes, dramatize, cut exposition, cut summary—but it can be misguided advice. Good prose almost always requires both showing *and* telling, scenes *and* summary, the two basic components of creative prose.

First for some definitions:

Scenes are episodes that occur within a specific time and place, just like in films, and they give the reader a sense of events transpiring in real time. At their best, scenes allow us to enter the action, feel the emotions of the characters, empathize, and even to enjoy catharsis. They grab our attention and let us know that what is being conveyed matters. Here's an example:

> Pinned to the reclining dentist chair with her mouth stretched into the shape of a silent scream, Margaret realized, even before the Novocain took hold, that Dr. Verbsky would make the perfect father for her yet-to-be-conceived child. "Open wider, please," he said, leaning in, his gloved fingers delicately wielding silvery tools, his breath faintly spicy from lunch, a lunch that Margaret had skipped because she didn't want Dr. Verbsky to see pieces of it lodged between her teeth. The plastic-covered light sent rays of revelation into her squinted eyes. Margaret sensed, without quite feeling, Dr. Verbsky's knuckles pressing into her numb lips. Was it really true that dentists had the highest suicide rate among professionals, she wondered. Was that because they couldn't bear causing pain every day, or did potential suicides tend to become dentists?

In the above scene we are in a specific time (the illusory fictional clock is ticking away) and place (Dr. Verbsky's office, the dentist's chair). We're not learning about a series of root canal appointments, or a series of possible donors, only this one. Even when Margaret reflects on dentists and suicide, she is reflecting *in the moment, within the scene* and not in some vague narrative ether. We have only the moments that pass under that bright light. The writer uses a scene here because this is the moment in which Margaret makes her choice and therefore it has dramatic import. Though we don't know when or how she'll ask Verbsky to cooperate, we expect that when she does she'll do it in a scene, not a summary.

As you can see, scenes are essential to bring a work to life, yet, for the fiction writer or memoirist, creating *only* scenes can rob a work of context and meaning. A work comprised of scenes alone, especially a long work, can be a welter of dramatic renderings, many of which provide information that doesn't deserve to take up that much space. If everything is written as a scene, how does the reader know where the emphasis lies? Where is the opportunity for narrative reflection? And how does a writer move between scenes without enormous gaps? Thus the need for summary.

Summaries are the material in between scenes—they may contain background exposition, description that doesn't occur in a specific scene, interior thoughts, events that happen repeatedly or that are being recounted in a compressed fashion, and narrative commentary or reflection. A distinctive voice, that elusive quality we all desire as writers, often comes through best in summary. Here's an example:

> For several weeks Margaret had been reviewing all the men in her limited sphere, wondering whom she might approach as a possible sperm donor. She considered and rejected the trainer at her gym—too judgmental

about her body; the mechanic at the Ford garage who reminded her she was about to go off warranty—friendly but too short; and a college classmate who'd recently been divorced and had asked to be her friend on Facebook—too needy and possibly complicated. It was only when she went to her third root canal appointment that the answer became clear.

Both the scene and summary above tell us about Margaret's desire to find a biological father for her child. They both introduce us to her thought patterns and employ particular details, but in the summary, time has been compressed to encompass several weeks of consideration. Without this summary we wouldn't know as much about Margaret, the nature of her search for a sperm donor, or the unpromising list of possible donors—all of which tell us something about her limited social connections. We've also learned how recently she began the search process. The summary gives context to the scene in the doctor's office. The Margaret and Verbsky scene can proceed without the summary but the summary has enriched the scene, and vice versa.

Perhaps the reason telling has gotten such a bad name is that the craft term *summary* is often confused with the kinds of summaries we all had to write in middle school, synopsis and recapitulation. I always resented the summary at the end of the famous five-paragraph essay. Couldn't the reader remember what I'd written just a paragraph or two ago? And I still resent, as most readers would, a narrative in which the author explains what a scene has already made obvious—*reporting* rather than *evoking* the most significant events in the characters' lives. That sort of summarizing leaves the reader far removed from the action and emotions of the characters; it's alienating and dull. The trick with summary is determining when it's a distancing shortcut or unnecessary explication, and when it's a chance to

deepen themes, reveal character, and express an author's distinctive voice.

Once you have learned the potential of both scene and summary, you must decide which is called for when, and how to slide between them gracefully. Understanding and making effective use of the interaction of scene and summary within stories, novels, essays, and memoirs is very important to the success of the whole work. The intention of this book is to help you to create vibrant scenes and essential summaries, and to find the connections and balance between them.

Showing:
Making Vibrant Scenes

*W*hy do we read fiction and memoirs? Although many creative works contain useful information, that isn't their primary draw. If we simply want information, we can go to a dictionary or a history book or search online. We read creative prose because we want to be transported out of our own skins into the lives of others—we read to expand our emotional awareness, not just our factual understanding of the world. In literature, this is accomplished through the use of scenes. As I said in the introduction, but will repeat here because of its great importance: To be truly engaged in the lives of characters, events must be *dramatized* rather than simply reported; for dramatic impact we must be grounded in place and experience the illusion of real time passing, which only occurs in scenes. We must live the moment along with the characters, *especially moments of change.* And change—in characters, in circumstances, and in the perceptions of readers—is the essence of narrative. While summaries may supply the connective tissue, scenes are the blood and breath of fiction, narrative essays, and memoir. In other words, most works show *and* tell but the showing is absolutely essential.

A Note on Intention

As writers we often experience getting lost in the middle of a story, essay, chapter—or, in some cases, book—we're writing. We aren't so much looking for a way out as for a way in, seeking a clear definition of the whole that will enable us to make each part contribute. The cure for this is to analyze our intentions. It works for the whole chapter or book or story, but right now we're concentrating on scenes, so I'll just address intention in scenes. Before you write a scene, or after you've written an initial draft of it—depending on your preferred manner of composition—get in the habit of taking a moment to contemplate what you wish to accomplish in that scene. Ask yourself the following questions: What is this scene really about? What is at stake in the scene? How does this scene contribute to the piece as a whole? Forcing yourself to articulate your own intentions for a scene is hard because it requires you to be analytical when you might prefer to be intuitive and "creative." Yet both are necessary parts of the writing process.

Once you have established a clear intention you will know what needs to be cut, what should stay, what should be developed further, or even if the scene should be there at all. Establishing intention is vital to both the composition and the revision process.

Chapter 1

THE PURPOSE OF SCENES

Scenes are never there just for "color"; they have several very important jobs to do. Most scenes don't meet all of the criteria listed below but they should meet at least a few. Scenes are used to:

- create an emotional connection between character/s and reader
- dramatize events
- move action/plot forward
- introduce or intensify conflict
- build suspense
- create change over time
- introduce or reveal character
- introduce themes
- establish mood
- provide resolution

CREATING AN EMOTIONAL CONNECTION

Scenes create an emotional connection for the reader by making characters and events seem real, and by giving characters recognizable, though complex, emotions. The "real" feeling comes from the reader going through the experience *with* the character as it's happening in time, complete with sensory detail.

For example, if you read that Sally broke her ankle you think, too bad, without feeling anything. On the other hand, if you read a *scene* in which Sally, on her first day of teaching kindergarten, gives in to a little girl's request that she try the slide, most of the elements on the above list can be accomplished:

> Sally lands at the bottom of the twisty yellow slide; she hears a grinding pop in her left ankle as she lurches to the gravel. "Shit!" she yelps before she can stifle herself. She's fallen forward on her hands and knees. Pebbles cut her palms and her ankle feels ablaze. The little girl with crooked glasses who asked her to go down the slide stands there openmouthed. Sally thinks about the tippy espadrilles she insisted on wearing that morning because they were new; she groans and lays her head in the playground dust.

You wince (I hope) in sympathy at Sally's pain and the embarrassment this is going to bring her. You've connected to Sally as a person because the scene has been rendered dramatically rather than reported. As you can see, the purposes listed above work synergistically. The *dramatized* event moves *the story action forward* as a broken ankle due to an overzealous attempt to appear playful or to please a student—not to mention yelling *shit* in front of a kindergartener—will surely complicate Sally's life as a new teacher, and the action itself *reveals an aspect of Sally's character*—she's a pleaser but she's also impulsive. The scene creates immediate *internal conflict* caused by pain and shame, as well as the possibility of *future conflict*—between Sally and the school administration and perhaps a parent, not to mention struggling with a cast. The scene even *creates suspense* as we wonder what will be the repercussions of Sally's actions. *Change over time* has taken place—Sally's situation and perhaps our impression of her have changed over the course of the scene.

Showing & TELLING

Mood has been established as one of only semiseriousness— Sally's expletive, the silliness of an adult breaking an ankle on a playground slide, and the ridiculous tippy espadrilles all combine to suggest that the story might be ironic or perhaps playful. The scene does not contain *resolution* (a satisfying outcome to a problem raised by the story). That would have to occur further along in the narrative, but the scene could *introduce themes* that will be developed later. What themes might these be from the little we know? That depends on the writer's intention—what he wishes to emphasize as central to the *meaning* of the story. (Theme is not plot; theme is what the story or essay is about on its deepest level.) Possible themes, if this story continued, could include something as banal as "look before you leap" or something more complicated such as "it took an accident for Sally to discover that she wasn't cut out to be a kindergarten teacher and that she needed to keep searching for her true calling."

WHAT ABOUT PLOT?

I mentioned above that scenes move the action forward. To clarify: *Action* refers to the events that happen in a scene and in the narrative as a whole—this happened, then that happened. *Plot,* however, is action with a *cause-and-effect relationship*—this happened *because* that happened. E.M. Forster's famous explanation for action vs. plot goes like this:

> Action = the king died and then the queen died.
> Plot = the king died and then the queen died of grief.

So when we talk about scenes moving the action forward in a piece we can also say that scenes move the plot forward, as long as the events have a causal relationship. Poor Sally went down the twisty slide and broke her ankle. That's action. Sally got in trouble with the principal and lost her job *because* after breaking her ankle she swore in front of a kindergartener. That's plot. You want to make sure you use scenes rather than summary whenever you are writing about events that are particularly important to the plot. You could summarize Sally driving to school that day (action), but you want a scene for the ankle breaking and the later confrontation with the principal because of their importance to Sally's life and the story.

Chapter 2

TYPES OF SCENES

You are now familiar with the various jobs that scenes do. Given those purposes, scenes can be categorized by types in which a particular job is dominant.

- scenes that lay the groundwork for later scenes
- scenes that introduce or develop conflict
- scenes that introduce or reveal characters
- turning point scenes
- suspense scenes
- flashback scenes
- resolution scenes

LAYING THE GROUNDWORK FOR LATER SCENES

A quiet scene that sets up later action in the story of Sally might occur earlier that morning when Sally is getting dressed and chooses her tippy espadrilles as footwear because they are new, even if they aren't the best shoes for teaching kindergarten (foreshadowing Sally's later poor judgment and setting us up for her bad landing at the bottom of the slide).

Jo Ann Beard's personal essay "The Fourth State of Matter" concerns an ordinary day turned horribly wrong when a foreign student commits a mass shooting in the department where Beard works at the University of Iowa. In an early scene in the piece, Beard has a woman come to her house to get rid of invading squirrels. In the scene they discuss when to euthanize Beard's beloved but failing old collie, as well as the frantic phone calls from Beard's husband who is in the process of leaving her and wants her to comfort him. ("You call him back and I'm forced to kill you," Caroline, the squirrel catcher, jokes.) In the midst of the discussion, there is a lot of chasing of squirrels and squirrels shrieking when caught. None of the action in this scene is directly linked to the shooting spree (I've never understood the use of such a cheerful-sounding word as *spree* in this context) at the university. There is no cause and effect, for instance. Yet the inclusion of this scene sets up important parallels to what will follow (the panic of the squirrels and the panic of the victims of the shooting, the joking talk of killing the husband and the real discussion of euthanizing the dog, etc.). It establishes themes of life and death. It also reveals important information about the narrator's character and concerns. It functions well as a setup for the extraordinary, terrible events that are the focus of the piece.

To lay the groundwork for future scenes in your own work, consider the possibilities for *foreshadowing* major events to come, through references or parallels that will have greater meaning when those more momentous scenes occur. To use an extreme example, if someone is going to fall off a cliff, perhaps in an earlier scene she stumbles off a step, or the cliff comes up seemingly casually in conversation.

CONFLICT SCENES

Despite yoga and meditation, anger management classes, marriage counseling, and spiritual retreats, despite the fact that most of us avoid it when possible, that which we say we don't want in our own lives, *conflict* is exactly what we want in our *scenes.* Conflict creates reader interest. Conflict drives plot.

There are numerous kinds of literary conflict, historically broken down into categories such as Man against Man, Man against Society, Man against Fate, Man against Nature, and Man against Self (internal conflict). Conflict can take place on a grand scale, such as in Stephen Crane's story "The Open Boat" in which shipwrecked men are in conflict with the sea and their fates. Or it can occur on a smaller, more personal level, as in a scene of an argument between partners. Either way, it involves characters having desires and those desires being thwarted by obstacles of some kind. These desires and the obstacles thrown in their way create *narrative tension.* If you want your readers to keep reading, you'll have to deliver narrative tension.

In Amy Tan's novel *The Joy Luck Club,* a daughter and her mother are in constant conflict. It boils over in one scene after the daughter has flubbed a piano recital by not practicing. The conflict in this scene is overt, direct, much of it carried through the dialogue. It begins when the mother tells her daughter it is time for practice.

> "I'm not going to play anymore," I said nonchalantly. "Why should I? I'm not a genius."
>
> She walked over and stood in front of the TV. I saw her chest was heaving up and down in an angry way.
>
> "No!" I said, and now I felt stronger, as if my true self had finally emerged. So this was what had been inside me all along.
>
> "No! I won't!" I screamed.
>
> She yanked me by the arm, pulled me off the floor, snapped off the TV ... She lifted me up and onto the hard bench. I was sobbing by now, looking at her bitterly. Her chest was heaving even more and her mouth was open, smiling crazily as if she were pleased I was crying.

"You want me to be someone that I'm not!" I sobbed. "I'll never be the kind of daughter you want me to be!"

"Only two kinds of daughters," she shouted in Chinese. "Those who are obedient and those who follow their own mind. Only one kind of daughter can live in this house. Obedient daughter!"

"Then I wish I wasn't your daughter. I wish you weren't my mother," I shouted. As I said these things I got scared. It felt like worms and toads and slimy things crawling out of my chest, but it also felt good, as if this awful side of me had surfaced, at last.

"Too late change this," said my mother shrilly.

There are actually several forms of conflict going on in this scene—the overt conflict of a daughter not wanting to practice piano when her mother wants her to, a daughter resisting her mother's authority and her mother's image of the perfect Chinese-American child, and a daughter fighting to break free of the old country traditions of her Chinese-born mother. You could say that the daughter's desire is for independence and the mother's desire is for her daughter to submit to her authority and to display virtuosity as a pianist. In any case, the conflict is apparent on the page.

Conflict in a scene can be less overt, more hidden, as in Raymond Carver's story "Are These Actual Miles?" in which a husband and wife have fallen on financial and marital hard times. The husband has sent his wife out to sell their car to a used car dealer before someone "slaps a lien on" it. He knows that she'll be the more effective seller. But she spends hours on her hair and face and clothing, dragging out her preparations, and he's worried that the used car lots will close for the day.

Leo stands in the bedroom doorway and taps his lips with his knuckles, watching.

"You're making me nervous," she says. "I wish you wouldn't just stand," she says. "So tell me how I look."

"You look fine," he says. "You look great. I'd buy a car from you anytime."

"But you don't have money," she says, peering into the mirror. She pats her hair, frowns. "And your credit's lousy. You're nothing," she says. "Teasing," she says and looks at him in the mirror.

Carver has created a number of levels of conflict within this scene. There is the simple conflict of the husband worrying that the wife won't get out of the house in time to sell the car. The wife takes her time, perhaps to punish the husband for degrading her with the task ahead. The greater conflict within the scene is the state of the marriage; the wife has lost all respect for her husband and is going to make him pay, even if she uses the cruel disclaimer "teasing." Unlike in the Amy Tan scene in which a child screams "I don't want to be your daughter," the wife is less overt about her emotions and her motives, but the message comes through to the reader.

Note that Carver has raised the tension in the scene through a simple gesture: Leo stands watching, tapping his knuckles against his lips, surely a sign of unease. The author could have stuck in a line *telling* us that Leo was nervous, but this gesture *shows* Leo's state of mind via his body language. It draws the reader further into the scene, allowing us to observe and deduce Leo's state of mind for ourselves. It's usually more vivid and more affecting when emotional states can be denoted by action or dialogue in scenes rather than by authorial telling. It's true that Carver has told the reader that Leo "is worried" about the lots closing before Toni gets out of the house, but the physical gesture of Leo tapping his knuckles against his lips works nicely to indicate nervousness about deeper issues that Leo may not have acknowledged to himself yet.

Though not every scene has to contain conflict there must be narrative tension in the piece as a whole. For instance, you could have a scene of a couple falling in love; it fulfills a purpose in the overall story and doesn't hold apparent conflict. But if the whole story is simply about how much in love these two are, with no opposition or troubles, it wouldn't be a particularly interesting story. If the young lovers were, like Romeo and Juliet, breaking the lines of a family feud, or if one is married, or must go to war, or can't marry because he has to stay home and care for aging parents, then you have conflict. Without conflict, no matter how lovely the language or appealing the characters, their real natures won't be tested or revealed; the story will be robbed of the opportunity for revelation or change and the reader will end up disappointed.

Even in the most meditative and philosophical of creative nonfiction, such as in Annie Dillard's *Pilgrim at Tinker Creek*, conflict has its place. In her chapter "The Present," when Dillard stops at a roadside gas station and pets a puppy while drinking coffee, conflict arises between her desire to fully experience the moment and the human impulse to analyze and thereby break the spell of the now.

> The air cools; the puppy's skin is hot. I am more alive than all the world. This is it, I think, this is it, right now, the present, this empty gas station, here, this western wind, this tang of coffee on the tongue, and I am patting the puppy, I am watching the mountain. And the second I verbalize this awareness in my brain, I cease to see the mountain or feel the puppy. I am opaque, so much black asphalt. But at the same second, the second I know I've lost it, I also realize that the puppy is still squirming on his back under my hand. Nothing has changed for him. He draws his legs down to stretch the skin taut so he feels every

fingertip's stroke along his furred and arching side, his flank, his flung-back throat.

Notice the level of detail in this scene, which contains no dialogue and no more action than a woman patting a puppy at a gas station. Dillard develops the sensory details that pin her to the moment—the puppy's skin is hot, the air is cool, she tastes the tang of coffee on her tongue. Those grounding details make her fall from the experience of living in the moment all the more dramatic. Once self-awareness kicks in, she ceases to "see the mountain" or "feel the puppy." She is "opaque, black asphalt." Yet the puppy continues to live in the moment, as dogs do, and therefore Dillard offers another form of conflict—not only do humans analyze themselves out of experience but they've lost an animal's ability to experience life directly.

For those scenes that do contain external rather than only internal conflict, the conflict can be modulated. Not every conflict scene has to be earth-shatteringly intense; in fact, readers would become exhausted and perhaps even numb if all scenes offered only the constant barrage of (usually violent) conflict that Hollywood blockbuster movies provide. There would be no room for character development if all scenes were devoted to car chases or shoot-'em-ups or fireball explosions. And the same is true for character-based literary works. If in every scene characters are screaming at each other, the same numbing effect takes over.

To reiterate: Conflict in scenes can be large and obvious, devious and indirect, or philosophical and internal. It drives and enlivens scenes. Scenes without any form of conflict can still be useful—they can serve as setup for conflicts to come, for instance. But if they don't serve a purpose that ultimately moves the *entire piece* forward in a significant way, perhaps they shouldn't be scenes at all.

CONFLICT DEVELOPMENT

Because movies are composed entirely of scenes with no summary save for the occasional voice-over, I'm going to track conflict establishment and development in a popular film for the sake of simplicity. In the movie *Juno*, the central conflict is quickly established when the teenager Juno, swigging on an enormous jug of Sunny D, enters a store, uses another (we know from the clerk) home pregnancy test, and realizes that she is, in fact, pregnant. After a brief scene in which she pretends to hang herself with a licorice rope on her walk home, there's a scene in which Juno calls her friend Leah and they discuss the pregnancy and what she should do. Juno decides (temporarily, it turns out) to have an abortion. The central conflict (the pregnancy) has been introduced quickly and developed further in the phone call scene—the decision to have an abortion is filled with conflict. In a later scene, we watch Bleeker, Juno's friend and the unsuspecting father of the baby, getting dressed to run with the track team. This scene introduces character but not conflict, as does a scene in which we meet Juno's father, stepmother, and half-sister. A later scene further develops the conflict when Juno goes for her appointment at the abortion clinic and encounters a protesting classmate who tells her the baby already has fingernails. This increases Juno's inner conflict. Inside the abortion clinic all Juno sees and hears are fingernails scratching and tapping. She runs out—there will be no abortion. Further development occurs in the following scenes:

> Leah suggests they find an adoptive family through the
> *Penny Saver*
> Juno tells her parents about the pregnancy
> Juno tells Bleeker that she's pregnant
> Juno meets the prospective adoptive parents
> Juno and Bleeker have a falling out

> Juno and the adoptive father become friends/he flirts
> with her
> The future adoptive father decides to leave his wife

And so on. Not all of these scenes focus on conflict. Some develop character and subplot. But overall the movie continues to add complications until Juno decides to give the baby away to the soon-to-be-single adoptive mother anyway, goes through the birth, and comes to see that Bleeker is both her friend and her beloved.

Throughout the film, entirely through the use of scenes (and a few voice-overs), conflicts are introduced, developed, and in the end resolved.

A literary example of conflict introduction via scene and the continuing development of that conflict in other scenes can be found in Flannery O'Connor's story "A Good Man Is Hard to Find." In the first scene, over breakfast a family discusses driving to Florida on vacation the next day. The grandmother wants them to go elsewhere. She mentions The Misfit, a murderer on the loose, in an attempt to get her way, but it doesn't work. The grandmother's desires conflict with those of her son, his wife, and two kids. Smaller conflicts include the grandmother's annoying personality and the two nasty kids who mock her.

The family sets out for Florida, the grandmother hiding her forbidden cat in a basket under her valise on the floor. They stop at a restaurant where the subject of The Misfit comes up again and the general untrustworthiness of the world is discussed with the restaurant owner. From the tone of the conversation it becomes clear there's conflict between the owner and his wife who works as the waitress. Although it doesn't directly bear on the conflicts for the main characters, it adds to the thematic threads. Back in the car the grandmother tricks her son (untrustworthiness again) into taking a turnoff onto a dirt road to go look at an old plantation, but en route she suddenly realizes she's confused its location—the plantation is in another state. In her surprise and shame she upsets the valise, the hidden cat jumps out of its basket and onto the driving son's neck, and they crash their car (more conflict). Some frightening men appear on the road and the conflict (and suspense) builds: They are stuck in the middle of nowhere and strange men are bearing down on them. The conflicts have been heightened and the stakes raised: The family's survival is at risk now; the conflict is no longer who will get his way about where to go on vacation.

In the final scene it becomes clear that the men are led by The Misfit, whose arrival has been foreshadowed throughout. Foreshadowing can increase conflict, as it adds to the underlying tension. All of the conflicts are resolved when The Misfit's henchmen murder the father and son, then mother and daughter, and after a moment (according to some critics, of grace) in which the old lady, nearly delusional, calls him one of her own children, The Misfit shoots the grandmother. In this story the initial conflict raised in the first scene (the grandmother's desire to get her way) is followed by a series of conflict-filled scenes until the much larger final conflict (the family being threatened and then murdered by The Misfit and his henchmen). In O'Connor's larger design, the conflict between good and evil and life with or without grace provides a thematic structure to the story. It could also be said that O'Connor's ironic tone, which my synopsis doesn't capture, adds to the tension in the story. In any case, the story has introduced, developed, and increased conflicts throughout its scenes until the resolution; the conflicts begin as trivial and end up deadly.

Think about the conflicts operating in your own work. Do they develop as the piece moves on or do they remain static? What ways might you intensify and further complicate the initial conflicts? Does the resolution of these conflicts feel satisfying?

SCENES THAT INTRODUCE CHARACTER

Each of the conflict scenes in the Flannery O'Connor story also serve to introduce character. In the first scene we get a strong picture of the grandmother's pushy nature and in the next scene, in the car, we learn that she is also sly—she has hidden her cat in a basket on the floor. The old lady's daughter-in-law is described as having a face as "broad and innocent as a cabbage," a description that goes a long way toward revealing her character. The kids reveal themselves in the first scene through their dialogue: "If you don't want to go to Florida why dontcha stay at home?" asks the little boy and his sister says, "She wouldn't stay at home for a million bucks. She has to go everywhere we go." The mother might be innocent but the kids are already well versed in sarcasm and cruelty. The son's character is never revealed—he remains something of a cipher.

The development of conflict and character go hand in hand because conflict *reveals* character. Yet there can be scenes in which the primary purpose is to reveal character and conflict doesn't come into play. Obviously, there can't be too many scenes of this sort or the reader might lose interest. An example of such a scene might be Margaret (from the Doctor Verbsky scene in the introduction) shopping for baby clothes or bassinettes even before she's selected her sperm donor. If we pushed it, we could find conflict in that scene—the conflict between her desire for a child and her prospects for one at that moment—but the intention of that scene would be to display the intensity of her desire for a child rather than to take on the obstacles to her having one, and so the revelation of character is the primary job of the scene.

TURNING POINT SCENES

Turning points in the action or the character's emotions must be rendered in scenes rather than summary. Can you imagine Rhett

Butler's famous line "Frankly, my dear, I don't give a damn," in
Gone With the Wind relayed in summary instead of in the vivid
scene in which Scarlett finally decides she loves him but Rhett
has had enough and walks out on her?

In Herman Melville's classic story "Bartleby the Scrivener,"
a lot of initial summary describes the members of the narrator's
office, but when the narrator asks his (until this point accom-
modating) clerk, Bartleby, to do some copying, and Bartleby
shakes the narrator's little world by saying "I would prefer not
to," a scene conveys this turning point. After Bartleby's refusal,
the story has changed direction.

Turning points can be shown via actions, as when the teenage girl alone in her family's house in Joyce Carol Oates's story
"Where Are You Going, Where Have You Been?" walks out the
door to join the terrifying stalker Arnold Friend.

Turning points can occur without direct confrontation. A
turning point scene might be wholly internal, as when it leads
up to a character making an important decision or coming to
see the truth about a situation without necessarily voicing that
awareness. If Sally gets called to the principal's office and is
reprimanded and put on probation, and while the principal is
chastising her she decides to quit her job, this would be a turning point. There's been no open confrontation (though there's
plenty of conflict), Sally has said nothing, but the event has led
to her decision to quit—that's a turning point scene.

Think about what point in your narrative your protagonist
or narrator reaches a turning point. Your turning point scene—
and it must be a scene, not a summary—can show this change in
the character's life or consciousness through thoughts, action, or
dialogue. But it must grow naturally out of what comes before so
that the turning point is credible. In other words, if you're going
to show a girl walking out of her house to join a scary stalker,
you better have already shown us that this stalker has, through
terror and threats of reprisals on her family, broken this girl's

will. You want your readers to believe in the turning point, and they won't if it comes out of thin air.

SUSPENSE SCENES

Suspense is that nervous feeling of anticipation when we want to know what's going to happen next but we have to wait to find out. Suspense can be generated in a scene when the reader knows more than the character knows, as in all those teen slasher movies when the innocent party girl goes wandering down the dark hall at night and the audience thinks, *Don't open that door!* Of course, whenever there is a high level of danger threatening characters, the scene will be suspenseful as we wait to discover if they will survive. The whole genre of cliff-hangers developed out of the serialization of stories (and later movies) that used that kind of life-or-death suspense to keep the audience interested enough to wait for the next week's installment.

Suspense can also function in scenes that are not concerned with the character's survival. Scenes can create suspense by raising an open-ended question: Will the girlfriend be tempted by her boyfriend's best friend? Will the child pass the exam? Will Hamlet ever get over his indecision and take action to avenge his father's murder? Will the new stepmother win over the angry and resentful stepchildren? Will Joe get his promotion when he's called in to speak with his boss? Will the cop give you a ticket? If we're so engaged with the characters and the situation that we care about the answer, the suspense will compel us to read on.

On a more subtle level, suspense can be created when a child (or childlike adult) misinterprets adult action or conversation and makes the wrong assumption. In Ian McEwan's novel *Atonement*, thirteen-year-old Briony misinterprets an impassioned meeting between her older sister and a servant's son as a sexual assault. The reader understands what Briony doesn't; suspense is generated as readers wait to see what the consequences of Briony's mistaken and overimagined version of that meeting will be. This sort of suspense is very effective because it *shows* the reader information that a character doesn't know or understand—rather like the way the audience feels watching the girl open the door in a teen slasher film, though it may be other characters rather than the protagonist who will suffer, as in *Atonement*.

FLASHBACKS

Flashbacks are scenes (or fragments of scenes) that have occurred before the current time frame of the piece. They can interrupt ongoing scenes or be presented in their entirety separate from the ongoing action. Flashbacks allow you to *show* rather than tell background information via summary.

Flashbacks function much the way a glimpse of memory pops up while you are engaged in another action. If you were to trace your thoughts back you would probably find an association that prompted that memory. In writing, you want the flashback to have a connection to the ongoing or surrounding scenes. It shouldn't be random—there has to be a good reason to go into a flashback as it stops the ongoing action. Flashbacks should provide information essential to readers' understanding of the current scene. The payoff for including them must outweigh the cost of losing forward momentum. What might be gained/lost if we added a flashback to the brief scene of Sally on the slide—for instance, if, in the midst of hurtling down the playground slide Sally thinks back to an earlier, perhaps equally ill-fated slide incident from her own childhood? The flashback to that earlier event could signal that this one might not end so well (a flashback that foreshadows):

> When she was six Sally sat on a piece of waxed paper like the big kids did and traveled down the old metal slide in the Catholic School playground. It was too fast, way too fast, not fun at all—she'd wanted it to stop and then it did, abruptly. She'd slid right off the end of the slide to land with a thump on her back. The wind was knocked out of her and she couldn't catch her breath; she thought she was dying. And around her stood a ring of kids' faces, scared at first, then laughing when she caught her breath and immediately started crying. "Crybaby! Crybaby!" Their chant still rang in her head.

What do we gain from including this flashback? We realize that Sally has a history of bad luck with slides and that she's either an optimist or someone who doesn't learn from the past. We also learn that she has a history of humiliation. Instead of that particular flashback, we might choose to insert one about an instance of breaking a bone when she was little (a memory of physical pain) after the line about her ankle being ablaze, or we could insert it at the end when she's in the dust. Or, alternatively, the flashback could appear after Sally "thinks about the tippy espadrilles she insisted on wearing because they were new" and focus on a memory of buying new shoes as a child, a memory that reveals why new shoes are so important to her.

Whichever place and whatever memory the writer chooses to insert as flashback would depend on the writer's *intention* for the piece—emphasizing Sally's history of humiliation, or physical pain, or childish excitement over new shoes. One thing's for certain—the writer *cannot* insert all three and probably shouldn't insert two. What would happen might look like this:

> Sally reaches the top step and plops onto the yellow plastic slide. Her polyester skirt acts like lubricant and she picks up speed rapidly. When she was six Sally sat on

a piece of waxed paper like the big kids did and traveled down the old metal slide in the Catholic School playground. It was too fast, way too fast, not fun at all—she'd wanted it to stop and then it did, abruptly. She'd slid right off the end of the slide to land with a thump on her back. The wind was knocked out of her and she couldn't catch her breath; she thought she was dying. And around her stood a ring of kids' faces, scared at first, then laughing when she caught her breath and immediately started crying. "Crybaby! Crybaby!" Their chant still rang in her head.

Now, at Grover Cleveland Elementary School, on her first day of teaching, Sally lands at the bottom of the twisty yellow slide; she hears a grinding pop in her left ankle as she lurches to the gravel. "Shit!" she yelps before she can stifle herself. She's fallen forward on her hands and knees. Pebbles cut her palms and her ankle is ablaze.

Once, when she was seven, Sally fell out of Mrs. Gunfeld's apple tree and shattered her forearm. She lay on the ground wailing until her mother ran across two yards to pick her up. That night her father came home from work with a bunch of helium balloons and ice cream and admired her pink cast. Still, it hurt too much to sleep and the cast felt like wearing a cement block on the end of her arm. Her mother stayed up with her reading stories while she moaned and tossed in her bed.

There would be no balloons or pink casts this time. And she was supposed to start taking tango lessons tomorrow! The little girl with crooked glasses who had asked her to go down the slide stands there openmouthed. Sally thinks about the tippy espadrilles she insisted on wearing that morning because they were new; she used to love to shop for new shoes every fall, even if her mother insisted on sturdy, well-made running shoes when she wanted flats or Mary Janes. Only once had her mother allowed her to pick out shoes because they were pretty instead of practical. That was after her father decided to live with Mrs. Gunfeld and didn't come home anymore. Her mother drove to the mall in Kingston that Saturday ... (and so on) ...

Sally groans and lays her head in the playground dust.

Well, as you can see, there's a lot more backward motion than forward motion and the constant interruptions become irritating. Sure, we've learned a lot about Sally's background but we've lost our sense of the ongoing scene. The writer could filter in some of those other flashbacks elsewhere in the story—perhaps that night, when Sally has come back from the emergency room and is taking painkillers, or when she carries her now unneeded espadrille home in her bag. Taken all together, multiple flashbacks are confusing and counterproductive.

Besides the trap of overdoing them, flashbacks can be a problem if you don't know how to get in and out of them smoothly and "naturally." Here are some tips:

- Try not to use verbs such as "remember" or "recall," as in "Dave remembered the last time he'd run over a squirrel ... " to announce a flashback. "The last time Dave had run over a squirrel ... " functions fine without the verb "to remember" and is less obviously a device.

- A verb change is important. If you're writing your scene in the present tense, a simple shift to past tense lets us know we've moved back in time. ("When she was six Sally sat on a piece of waxed paper ...")

- If you're writing in past tense already, you need to establish a few uses of past perfect (Dave *had* driven ... he'd smashed ...) to establish that you're referring to a time in the distant past, preceding the past you're writing in.

- Use time markers to help notify readers that they are entering a flashback, such as "When she was six" above, or "then" or "last year" or "Saturday" or "when she was little" and so on.

- To return from the flashback, draw your readers' attention to the ongoing action again. For example: "In the Honda on I-80, Dave saw in the rearview mirror that the squirrel he thought he'd hit was now running into the brush at the side of the road." Or, "Lying in the dust at the base of the yellow plastic slide, Sally glances up at ..." Besides the tense change, the color of the slide—the one in the flashback was metal, this one is yellow plastic— provides a marker to keep the reader aware of which time frame we're in.

- There's nothing wrong with using words such as *now* or *here* or *today* to tip off your reader about a return to the ongoing scene, as in, "Sally struggled up now and hobbled to a bench, squelching the desire to cry the way she had ... " The important thing is that you keep your reader located in time; it's very frustrating for readers when they can't figure out what's happening when and they're likely to give up on your story.

- Weigh whether or not what you're conveying in a flashback is important enough to require a remembered *scene,* or if it could be conveyed by *summary* instead—this will be easier for you to decide after you've read Section II on telling (see page 94).

RESOLUTION SCENES

In a resolution scene, a conflict that has driven the narrative comes to some kind of a conclusion. If the conflict is important, you don't want to resolve it by reporting the outcome through summary. You'll need to show it.

In *Romeo and Juliet*, Romeo mistakenly believes that Juliet is dead and so kills himself; she then awakens and, seeing Romeo dead, kills herself. These deaths resolve the young couple's inability to be together in life as well as the conflict between the two lovers' warring families. Because it is a play and plays are made up only of scenes, it has to be rendered in a scene, but if the story were contained in a novel, Shakespeare would have written this as a scene. To report rather than evoke the deaths of the major characters would be to cheat the reader.

Shakespeare often used death, in fact multiple deaths, as a form of resolution—it is a venerable mode for tying up a story but it has been greatly overused since Shakespeare's time in many books and films. Think of the movies *Bonnie and Clyde* or *Easy Rider* or Flannery O'Connor's story "A Good Man Is Hard to Find," all of which resolve their stories with shootings. Not all violent endings involve shootings, of course. Think of the destruction of the whaling ship (and Captain Ahab) by the great white whale in Melville's *Moby-Dick*. Now there's an original ending, even if violent!

Nonviolent death scenes make a regular appearance in resolving books and movies such as *Terms of Endearment* and deathbed scenes have become a cliché as well.

Mysteries, of course, often begin with a death and the resolution comes with the solving of the mystery in a resolution scene.

Other forms of resolution can include the happy ending or "making up"—spouses, lovers, business partners, siblings, parents, and children overcome their differences in a resolution scene. (Think of *A Midsummer Night's Dream*, romance fiction, or the old Hollywood formula of "Boy gets girl, boy loses girl, boy gets girl again." The trick with the "happy ending" resolution is that it can't be sentimental or forced. The scene of the resolved difference must be believable; it must grow naturally out of the characters and actions that precede it and must not feel tacked on. If you write something along the lines of "Suddenly Marie realized that all her fights with her parents meant nothing; she truly loved them after all. She picked up the phone to call home ..." your readers are not going to be very satisfied. Happy resolutions, just as violent ones, must be earned by what comes before. In Marie's case, you better have created events that catalyze her turnaround before the resolution occurs or no one is going to believe it.

As an instructor in writing programs with mixed-age populations, I often saw what I came to call "A Doll's House" story (referring to Ibsen's play) in which a woman gets fed up and finally leaves her abusive or smothering or controlling husband. The resolution comes with a scene of the heroine walking out the door, ending the relationship. I don't mean to belittle the importance of such life-changing events for the writers, but any resolution scene used too often without sufficient variation loses its impact for the reader and risks becoming cliché, as with too many deathbed scenes. Even if the stories were varied, the resolutions weren't. A cliché resolution is a bad resolution.

Resolutions don't always have to come with the finality of death or happy endings or divorce; resolutions can be less obvious, more subtle. In fact, it could be argued that the real resolution in *Easy Rider* precedes the shooting of the two motorcyclists; the *emotional* resolution occurs when the Peter Fonda character tells the Dennis Hopper character, shortly before their

murders, that they've "blown it"—their drug money-fueled trip
has not been about freedom after all. From this standpoint, the
shootings end the movie but the scene of the realization *resolves*
the paradox of their trip.

In Chekhov's famous story "The Lady With the Pet Dog," a
cynical ladies' man seduces an unhappy wife vacationing alone
in the resort town of Yalta but then finds to his astonishment
that he has fallen in love with her. In the restricted mores of pre-
revolutionary, upper-class Russian society, neither can leave
their marriages without bringing ruin to all involved. The resolution scene is one in which the two lovers, who live in different
cities, have a brief rendezvous (they've continued to see each
other over the many years since they first met). In this scene they
delude themselves into thinking they'll find a solution to their
inability to be together. We know that they won't find a solution—the resolution comes in our witnessing, via this resolution
scene, their love and hope continuing despite the odds. The
resolution here is not an obvious ending, as the affair will most
likely continue; the resolution occurs when the reader comes to
understand the deep change within the formerly cynical protagonist, the limits society puts on their love, and the enduring
nature of their connection.

Another gentle resolution scene can be found in Raymond
Carver's story "Cathedral" in which a man who resents a visit
by his wife's old friend, a blind man, comes to see past his own
biases when he helps the blind man "see" a cathedral by draw-
ing one while moving the blind man's hand. The problem—the
narrator's resentment and bias—has been transcended in this
resolution scene.

Resolution scenes must fit the work that precedes them—if
the work is highly dramatic we expect a dramatic resolution
scene—for instance, a critical battle in a war story; if the work
is small and personal, as in "Cathedral," then the resolution
should be quiet as well. If your whole story is about difficulties

in personal relationships, you probably don't want to resolve it by having the character walk out the door and get hit by a truck. That won't be a satisfying resolution, just a resolution. Satisfaction for your reader comes from your showing a believable, well-earned (in the sense that it grows out of the events that precede it) outcome that is original, not cliché.

Chapter 3

SCENE STRUCTURE

$\mathcal{S}$cenes, just like books, stories, and essays, have beginnings, middles, and ends. You must find a way to get into a scene (beginning), accomplish the work of the scene (middle), and exit gracefully (ending).

SCENE BEGINNINGS

Scenes can begin "at the beginning"—introducing a character or situation with scene-setting description first, or starting the action with an initial event that catalyzes the scene, such as the old Western standby: A stranger rides into town. Scenes also can begin in the midst of action or dialogue, what's known as in medias res, as in Mark Schorer's story "The Face Within The Face":

> "Don't," Laura Newman said, too sharply for the occasion, and Robert, her husband, who had just begun to trace a light imaginary line along her smooth brown thigh, pulled his hand away and lay back on the sand.

This sentence starts both the scene and the story. It has begun in medias res—the author has provided no initial description, nor has he shown us the wife and husband arriving at the beach, walking across the hot sand, selecting their spot, or making chit-chat as the scene evolves. "Don't," the wife says, too sharply, and the story starts right up with the fundamental conflict between these mates. Revelation of aspects of her character and Robert's—he "pulled his hand away and lay back"—and the unhappy dynamic between them have already begun to be revealed.

There's no rule about which way to start a scene—with a slow buildup from the beginning or in medias res—but your choice should fit the nature of the subject and the mood you wish to convey. Schorer wanted to establish the husband's desire for and rejection by his wife quickly; the story focuses on the husband's helplessness in the face of his wife's coldness and her terrible parenting because he is dazzled by her beauty. Starting in media res works here because it basically cuts to the chase. But you won't want to "cut to the chase" in all cases.

Eudora Welty, in her story "A Worn Path," begins a scene:

> It was December—a bright frozen day in the early morning. Far out in the country there was an old Negro woman with her head tied in a red rag, coming along a path through the pinewoods. Her name was Phoenix Jackson. She was very old and small and she walked slowly in the dark pine shadows ...

The scene continues; quite a few pages pass before we learn where Phoenix Jackson is headed and why (to get medicine for her sick grandson), but along the way we experience her many trials. Welty has chosen this slow buildup within the scene because it is appropriate to a story about the determination and endurance of an old African-American woman in the Jim Crow South. The slow buildup sets the appropriate *mood* and introduces *theme* (such as Phoenix's strength against odds). Whether you provide your reader with a slower introduction like Welty or jump right into a scene as Schorer did, it's important to keep in mind that you need to establish reader interest quickly. Interest can be established via immediate conflict, as in Schorer's scene in which the tension between husband and wife opens the piece. Welty attracts our interest more slowly, though still surely, as we become engaged with the quirky *character* of this old woman who announces, when she hears rustling in the brush as she walks:

> "Out of my way, all you foxes, owls, beetles, jack rabbits, coons, and wild animals! ... Keep out from under these feet, little bobwhites ... Don't let none of those come running my direction. I got a long way."

Then it is suspense that keeps us interested as we wonder about the nature of Phoenix's journey.

Themes of the larger work can be introduced and developed at any point in the scene—beginning, middle, or end. Schorer begins introducing his themes in the first sentence. Welty introduces hers with the name Phoenix (surely a symbolic name) and the many trials the old woman encounters as the scene continues.

SCENE MIDDLES

Once you've established reader interest and gotten your scene underway, the middle of the scene is where you intensify conflict, develop and reveal character, and move the action forward. Conflict intensifies as complications arise and the stakes are raised. Schorer intensifies the conflict in his scene by introducing the couple's thirteen-year-old son, who overhears his mother's words and says, "Don't what?" The conflict is further developed when we learn that the mother, observing her son, thinks "puberty" and shudders, displaying her dislike of her son. Two new sources of conflict are introduced when: (1) The father wants to bring home their son from boarding school to live with them and the wife doesn't, and (2) A noisy, grossly unattractive family settles in behind their towel. The mother's character has been further revealed—she rejects her son as well as her husband, and she is deeply judgmental about the noisy family. The action has moved forward because the arrival of the other family will become the catalyst for the story's final conflict between mother and son.

SCENE ENDINGS

Scene endings do not necessarily mean scene resolutions. You may want to leave a scene unresolved in order to create suspense or interest in the next scene. But all scenes, which, you remember, take place in a single place and span of time, must end. The ideal is to end a scene strongly; you don't want it to fizzle out.

Many writers exit a scene through the use of an image or lingering action that crystallizes the themes or events presented in the scene, as does Schorer in "The Face Within the Face." Schorer's extended scene on the beach ends not when Laura, the wife, says, "My God, let's go" after witnessing the other mother's messy professions of love for her own child, but with the image of David, Laura's son, lagging behind, riveted by the other mother's warm, sloppy, overbearing but demonstrative connection to her child. The story hasn't ended, just the scene, and the reader is left with that haunting image of David's longing, a longing that matches his father's, though at this point the father is still a slave to his wife's beauty and the son has already seen beyond it. This kind of ending stresses the themes of the story.

The travel writer Colin Thubron, in *Shadow of the Silk Road*, has a lovely way of ending scenes with lingering sensory details and images. After an evening spent in the company of construction workers in an Iranian village, he writes:

> Only by midnight did we curl under our quilts on the hard
> floor, the timber ceiling shifting with insects above us,
> and sleep to the mechanical pipe of winter cicadas from
> the orchards outside, and the howl of the village dogs.

The howling dogs leave us with the impression of desolation that the scene establishes. It *shows* the feeling of the place.

Occasionally writers end scenes on a line of dialogue, cutting off the reader's chance to hear a reply and magnifying the impact of the final line, while adding a degree of suspense—what would the response have been?

Thubron often uses this technique. In another section of *Shadow of the Silk Road*, he meets a young Uzbek student in a café and discusses with him religious radicalism and Uzbekistan's independence from the Soviet Union. The scene ends when the boy says,

> "We've become poorer with independence. Old families
> are even having to sell their Korans—lovely things, written on skin, some of them with feathered quills. People
> say things were better in the Soviet time. We young can't
> remember that." He presses a finger to his pulse. "But I
> think there is slavery in our blood."

Slavery in our blood—it's a powerful statement that gives a poignant closure to the conversation and the scene. A powerful line of dialogue at the end of a scene will linger, just as a compelling image does.

Occasionally writers end a scene with an action. The novelist Abby Frucht often punctuates a scene with an action that her protagonists observe. In *Licorice,* a novel about a town in which the residents are inexplicably disappearing, one scene ends with her heroine watching a female amateur magician pulling a purple balloon out of a spectator's pants. Another scene ends with a toucan shaking a toy telephone that rings—both odd yet fitting images for a novel in which reality has become skewed.

The placement of a final action gives it more weight than if it didn't end the scene. For instance, in the brief scene of Sally and the broken ankle, the scene doesn't end with Sally calling for help or breaking into tears or reflecting on all the troubles to come; the scene ends with her laying her head in the dirt—a sign of resignation and defeat. The emphasis, then, in that scene is Sally's mood after her accident rather than a diagnosis of her injury or whether or not the other teachers run to her aid or any other option that might occur. In a more plot-based work, as in a thriller, an action that ends a scene might be intended to create suspense or set up for further actions to come. Ending a scene with a car crash, for example, might create suspense by leaving the reader to wonder whether or not the characters survived.

Whether you use action, image, or a line of dialogue to end your scene, the ending is a form of punctuation, putting form to the scene, emphasizing themes, ending forward motion, asserting a rest before more scenes and summaries arrive. You don't want your scenes to piddle away. Though every single scene doesn't need to end with a flourish (and frequent use of weighty scene endings can become an obvious device), scenes that end with powerful imagery, dialogue, or action will reverberate in the reader's mind.

Chapter 4 _____

TOOLS OF THE SCENE TRADE

TIME—USING THE ILLUSION OF REAL TIME IN SCENES

Time is a human construct by which we identify and measure experience. "Live in the now" the philosophers and spiritual practitioners tell us, although the closest most of us come to living in "the now" are certain moments of heightened importance—a car accident, a moment of blissful love, in a compelling natural setting perhaps, or when we've achieved "flow"—that involvement in our activities that is so intense we "lose track of time." Many of us would love to experience that loss of time more often, but in writing scenes we must have complete awareness and control of time.

As noted earlier, summary can be used to condense time (in the sense of relaying many events quickly), while a scene expands it (by giving the impression of real time passing). But how do you deal with time *within* a scene?

Whether you have chosen to cast your scene in the past, present, or even future tense (and I'll talk more about tenses shortly), the fact of the matter is that there is always a clock running for the duration of a scene. This clock, of course, is not the same as the time it takes a reader to traverse the pages; it is the time that exists within the scene, in the lives of the characters, yet it is an illusory clock. We could hardly represent every moment and every action that occurs in that dentist's office with Margaret and Dr. Verbsky (from the Introduction). You wouldn't necessarily want to hear each time he told her to open wider or experience along with Margaret every time the hygienist poked the suction tube into her mouth or learn of the exact sensation of the vinyl-covered dentist chair as it met her backside any more than you would want to learn all those details, those moments, from a friend who was telling you about her own stint in the dentist chair. Writing a scene requires us to be extremely selective.

An old Ukrainian lady I knew once said of a gabby neighbor, "She begins every story with Adam and Eve." You don't want to begin every *scene* with Adam and Eve or your story would become an unrelenting and oppressive profusion of details and irrelevant events. So, when you create a scene the passing of time must be *represented,* it must be *manufactured,* rather than recorded realistically. You must select the actions and thoughts of the narrator and/or characters within a scene with sensitivity to the choices that will have the most impact, depending on your intention. If your purpose for your scene is to display a moment in which a character begins to fall in love, you'll choose different actions and a different illusion of time passing than if your intention is to display an incident in which a teenager gets in a dramatic argument with a teacher and walks out of high school. You might want to slow the passage of time as the two potential lovers watch each other's smallest gestures, and you might want to speed up time when the rebellious teen curses and stomps out of the building. The representation of time must suit the effect you're trying to create. (Just how this is done will be covered shortly.)

I used to ask students in beginning writing classes to jot down what happened in the first five minutes of the first day of class. Invariably, one teacher-oriented student would report on my actions at the head of the room as I took attendance, shuffled my papers, etc., while another student would write about what other students were doing (chatting, chewing gum) and a third would examine his own fears—would he know anyone else in class, would he write anything worthwhile, would he have to read his work aloud? I designed the exercise to highlight differences in point of view but it also made a good illustration of the need for *selection* in representing the passage of time. Students would think about the details their fellows had chosen to include or omit and just how many details and actions you could or should include in representing five minutes of time passing. To be sure, that selection varies depending on a writer's individual style—Alain Robbe-Grillet, in a book I suffered through in high school French class called *La Jalousie* (a play on words using jealousy and the French word for the venetian blinds the protagonist was always staring through), made time slow down to a maddening second-by-second tick as his protagonist watched lizards on a wall while being driven crazy by his obsessive jealousy.

Most of us won't want to run the risk of driving the reader mad by slowing time to that extent, but certainly there is room for variation. Let's look at some examples.

In Elizabeth Tallent's short story "No One's a Mystery," narrated by an eighteen-year-old girl riding with her married lover in his pickup, the tale takes place in one extended scene that could occur in ten minutes of real time (ellipses for the sake of brevity are mine).

> For my eighteenth birthday Jack gave me a five-year diary ... I was sitting beside him scratching at the lock ... when he thought he saw his wife's Cadillac in the distance, coming toward us. He pushed me down onto the dirty floor of the pickup and kept one hand on my head while I inhaled the musk of his cigarettes in the dashboard ashtray and sang along with Rosanne Cash on the tape deck. We'd been drinking tequila and the bottle

was between his legs, resting up against his crotch ... In
a curve of cloth his zipper glinted, gold.

The story moves via moment-by-moment observation and eventually dialogue, after we get going with the line about the diary, a device that starts the story and also serves to advance its themes. Interestingly, time is central to this story, which focuses on Jack and the protagonist's differing views of the future of her love for him, characterized by what they both think she'll write in her diary over the next five years. The tension in the scene comes from the gap between what Jack and the reader both know will happen (she'll move on) vs. what the teenage narrator imagines will be their future together.

Obviously, this is a story (and a scene) all about time in the larger sense, but the manner in which time is represented in the story is the *illusion* of events unfolding moment by moment. Remember that Elizabeth Tallent has made the choice of what to omit as well as what to include—she doesn't give us the shape of Jack's Adam's apple, for instance, but she does tell us (elsewhere) that there is a "compact wedge of muddy manure between the heel and the sole ..." of Jack's boot, a detail that transmits in few words the nature of Jack's work. And she gives us his zipper glinting *gold*, a detail that serves to glorify the crotch of this man who mentions in the scene that he has taught the narrator "something about sex."

If you want your scene to give the impression of real time passing at a natural pace, limit the amount of description so the scene doesn't get bogged down but make sure that every bit of description carries a lot of information. Choose your details for what they tell about the characters.

Time can slow down even further, a sort of verbal slow motion as in this galvanizing moment in Bernard Cooper's personal essay "Burl's" when he, a restless eight-year-old, is sent out to buy a newspaper from the vending machine in front of the café in which his parents are drinking coffee. Two broad-shouldered women in cocktail dresses approach (once again I've condensed the excerpt for brevity):

> The closer they came the shallower my breathing was. I blocked the sidewalk, an incredulous child stalled in their path ... the pages of the *Herald* fluttered in the wind. I felt them against my arm, light as batted lashes.
>
> The woman in pink shot me a haughty glance ... her red lipstick more voluptuous than the lips it painted. Rouge deepened her cheekbones ... jaw was heavily powdered, a half-successful attempt to disguise the telltale shadow of a beard.

Time nearly comes to a stop in this scene and the language reflects this grinding to a halt. Cooper's *breathing gets shallower,* he *blocked* the sidewalk, was *stalled* in their path, he stands *frozen* on the sidewalk. His perception of physical stimuli is heightened—he feels the pages of the newspaper rustling against his arm. A little further along in the scene he uses the time-stopping phrase *just as I noticed this* and describes himself reflecting on the sudden realization that any woman could be a man *"in the midst of traffic, with my parents drinking coffee a few feet away ... "* The whole scene contains no dialogue; it focuses on Cooper's mental gyrations as a very important moment—one that perhaps took only seconds in reality—is stretched, examined, experienced, and catalogued for its enormous significance by a young child already struggling with his sexual identity. The important thing to note here is Cooper's use of time-slowing verbs and details.

Time can also be speeded up, as is apparent in this scene from Michael Cunningham's novel *A Home at the End of the World* in which a teenager has just run into a sliding glass door:

Carlton reaches up curiously to take out the shard of glass that is stuck in his neck, and that is when the blood starts. It shoots out of him. Our mother screams. Carlton steps forward into his girlfriend's arms and the two of them fall together. Our mother throws herself down on top of him and the girl. People shout their accident wisdom. Don't lift him. Call an ambulance. I watch from the hallway. Carlton's blood spurts, soaking into the carpet, spattering people's clothes. Our mother and father both try to plug the wound with their hands, but the blood just shoots between their fingers. Carlton looks more puzzled than anything, as if he can't quite follow this turn of events. 'It's all right,' our father tells him, trying to stop the blood. 'It's all right, just don't move, it's all right.' Carlton nods and holds our father's hand. His eyes take on an astonished light. Our mother screams, 'Is anybody *doing* anything?' What comes out of Carlton grows darker, almost black. I watch. Our father tries to get a hold on Carlton's neck while Carlton keeps trying to take his hand. Our mother's hair is matted with blood. It runs down her face … He is gone by the time the ambulance gets here.

The sentences are short, mostly subject-action constructions, and the verbs are explosive and action-filled. Blood *shoots* out of Carlton. It *spurts*. The mother *screams*. She *wails*. Blood *runs* down her face. Carlton and his girlfriend *fall*. People *shout*. The verbs pile up just as the mother and girlfriend pile onto Carlton but the action outpaces his life. After this excerpt, time slows back down and the sentences stretch out again as the family lives with the consequences of Carlton's death.

Time then, in the sense of the clock ticking within the scene, must be appropriate to the action, mood, and tone of the scene; verbs and carefully selected details are key components in establishing action, mood, and tone. Slow time requires slow verbs and fast time requires lots of action. Time can also be altered by the inclusion of summary within a scene, but we'll talk more about that later, in Section III.

A NOTE ON TENSES

When writing scenes you have the choice of present tense, past tense, and (though used less often) shooting forward into future tense. Each tense influences the feel of the scene. Present tense adds immediacy—events are happening in the very moment they are being narrated ("I turn the corner and see Jerry lighting a trash barrel on fire"). The past tense and past perfect ("I turned the corner and saw Jerry had just lit a trash barrel on fire") give a bit of distance from events—they imply that the narrator is telling the story either soon or long after it happened. They provide breathing room for the teller of the tale and the reader. The past tense is used most often, even in moment-by-moment scenes, as in the excerpt from Bernard Cooper's "Burls" above. The past tense often flows more easily than the every-moment-is-now nature of present tense.

The future tense ("I will turn the corner and see my little brother Jerry lighting a trash barrel on fire") throws the reader out of the present or past action into events that have not yet happened. Much like a flashback, future tense interrupts the ongoing narrative. It can be useful, occasionally, in telegraphing information that will be important to the reader's understanding of the ongoing scene ("Years from now, Jerry will be sent to a maximum security penitentiary as an arsonist responsible for the deaths of many people"). It disrupts the linearity of the narrative and in so doing, it influences the reader's connection to the characters—knowing that Jerry is going to end up in prison will affect the way you think of Jerry now, even if he is only eleven years old.

As with flashbacks, it's important to weigh the costs of interrupting the narrative against the possible payoffs such as giving readers a sense of prescience and informing readers of events that will change the way they judge the "current" characters and action.

Often present tense is chosen when the author is narrating from a child's point of view, in an attempt to lend immediacy and a child's limited understanding or perspective. In this excerpt from Edward P. Jones's short story "The First Day," present and future tense come into play. The story, which recounts a child's introduction to elementary school and her illiterate mother's attempts to get her enrolled in a better school, begins with a shoot into the future of remarkable weight, before settling into present tense with a couple of jumps back to past tense to set up the day (the italics are mine):

> On an otherwise unremarkable September morning, *long before I learned to be ashamed of my mother*, she takes my hand and we set off down New Jersey Avenue to begin my very first day of school. I am wearing a checkered-like blue-and-green cotton dress, and scattered about these colors are bits of yellow and white and brown. My mother has uncharacteristically spent nearly an hour on my hair that morning, plaiting and replaiting so that now my scalp tingles.

The choice of present tense matches the child's innocent, limited experience—this is all new for her and she's taking it in, moment by moment. The jump into the future with the words "long before I learned to be ashamed of my mother" provides crucial ballast to this story, a tragic weight. There is an older consciousness that emerges just this once—one who knows the future relationship between mother and child, and permits the reader to understand the ramifications of entering school for this child—this "first day."

The present tense has other uses as well as mirroring the experience of children. Jo Ann Beard, in her essay "The Fourth State of Matter," (discussed earlier in the section on laying the groundwork for later scenes), uses the present tense to keep the reader in suspense. The present tense increases impact here because the reader, like the narrator, experiences the devastating news of the university shooting in unfathomable fragments:

> The first call comes at four o'clock. I'm reading on the bench in the kitchen, one foot on a sleeping dog's back. It's Mary, calling from work. There's been some kind of disturbance in the building, a rumor that Dwight was shot; cops are running through the halls carrying rifles. They're evacuating the building and she's coming over.

If you intend to relay shocking or confusing information to a character, to *show* that character's disjointed response, you might try using the present tense.

The essayist Brenda Miller uses the present tense to describe getting ready for a man in her essay "The Date." Of course she could have written the scene in past tense (the date had already happened when the author wrote this essay). She uses the present tense to emphasize the anxiety of adult dating by ticking off the moment-by-moment countdown of her nervous preparations:

> A man I like is coming to dinner. In two hours. The chicken is marinating and the house is clean, and if I take a shower now and get dressed I'll have an hour and half to sit fidgeting on my living room chair, talking to myself and the fish, whose water, of course, I've changed. "Make a good impression," I plead with him. "Mellow out." He swims

back and forth, avoiding my eyes, butting his pinhead against his bowl. I call my friend: Do I light candles?

How different this would feel if Miller had written "A man I like came for dinner ... The chicken was marinated and the house was clean." We've lost the countdown feeling of her nervousness. If your scene requires a moment-by-moment feel, consider using present tense.

You can play around with alternatives to see which tense works best for a particular scene. Compare these versions:

> Sally lands at the bottom of the twisty yellow slide; she hears a grinding pop in her left ankle as she lurches to the gravel.
>
> Sally landed at the bottom of the twisty yellow slide; she heard a grinding pop in her left ankle as she lurched to the gravel.
>
> Next week Sally will land at the bottom of the twisty yellow slide; she will hear a grinding pop in her left ankle as she lurches to the gravel.

The present tense fits if your intention is to emphasize the moment-by-moment immediacy of the accident. The past tense works well if immediacy is not as important as the actions and their consequences. The third version, in future tense, would be more effective if it were part of something larger—a scene containing a present or past framework from which the writer could jump into the future. On its own it doesn't make a lot of sense.

You can combine tenses as long as you're careful to keep the reader located in time. A scene could begin in the present or past, then jump into the future tense and return:

> Sally lands at the bottom of the twisty yellow slide; she hears a grinding pop in her left ankle as she lurches to

the gravel. "Shit!" she yelps before she can stifle herself. In just a few days, hobbling on crutches, she will be called onto the carpet by the principal, who will want to know if she thinks using vulgar language is appropriate for a kindergarten teacher at Grover Cleveland Elementary School. Right now, though, all she can think about is her ankle.

Notice that the future tense scene is located by the time marker "in just a few days" and the writer returns the reader to the current scene, in present tense, with the tag "Right now..." If you're going to combine tenses, be sure to use markers to avoid losing your reader.

A more elegant example of playing with tenses is contained in the first line of Gabriel García Márquez's *One Hundred Years of Solitude* : "Many years later, as he faced the firing squad, Colonel Aureliano Buendía was to remember that distant afternoon when his father took him to discover ice." The book covers many years in the history of a family, but those years are relayed in anything but a linear chronology. Nonetheless, Márquez, the Nobel laureate, uses time markers such as "many years later" and "that distant afternoon."

A Final Note on Tenses

You should not switch tenses *unless there is a reason to do so*, such as an effect you are after, like Márquez's mingling of past/present/future or, more simply, mixing a brief spate of present into past tense for heightened impact, or jumping back into the past to give background in the midst of a present-tense scene, as with flashbacks. Random jumping from one tense to another as in "He went downstairs and reaches for the orange juice" is both confusing and annoying to a reader.

MORE ON USING TIME TAGS

The easiest way (and a perfectly acceptable one) to locate the scene in a specific time is to use time tags such as *June first, 1963 ... One day ... Last Thursday ... Before we sat down for supper ... After she went into labor ... When the hike ended ...*

Here are some published time tags:

> Jo Ann Beard: "I've called in tired to work. It's mid-morning and I'm shuffling around in my long underwear ..."

> Edward P. Jones: "On an otherwise unremarkable September morning ..."

> Mary Clearman Blew: "December 1958. I lie on my back on an examination table in a Missoula clinic ..."

There are other, more complex ways of locating a scene in time than by using simple tags. Leslie Marmon Silko, in the story "Yellow Woman," lets us know that it is dawn with this sentence: "My thigh clung to his with dampness, and I watched the sun rising through the tamaracks and willows."

In the Silko example, the time marker "I watched the sun rising through the tamaracks ..." does more than one job. It not only tells us it is early morning, but it creates a picture for the reader, establishing setting. The reader sees what the narrator sees, and so we are drawn quickly into the scene. This is not to say that Jones or Beard or Blew won't draw us into their scenes with powerful description; they will. But whenever a description can do double duty (in this case locating us in time *and* place) without having to state the facts directly, the prose is particularly economical. It also is an example of "showing" rather than "telling" even though both methods of location in time occur within scenes.

If you decide to try a complicated method of locating your scene in time, make sure you haven't gotten so complex or lyrical that your marker misfires and your reader gets lost. If you write "They met in the shimmer of falling light in cascades of iridescent joy," your reader might long for the old newspaper where-what-when-how-why style.

PLACE, OR SETTING

As I said earlier, all scenes require a time and a place. But place in its broader sense, setting, can include the historical epoch as well as the physical location, the weather as well as the geography or topography. Setting encompasses all aspects of the milieu in which your scene occurs. One reason for working on setting is to create a credible experience for the reader—to make the scene feel real—but setting can and should do more than just establish a believable background to the action of the scene. Setting can have symbolic meaning, it can reveal aspects of character, establish mood and tone. Compare these two scenes:

> A) My father turns the frosted Buick off the two-lane blacktop and down a long, badly ploughed driveway. Far from any neighbors, with dusk falling, my grandparents' house looks uncared for; the porch is buckling, the siding needs paint, sagging sheds slump against the drifts of snow. Bare trees loom over the house, their branches clawlike against the darkening sky. I shiver and grip my father's hand for comfort but when I look up at him I see that an expression of fear and sorrow contorts his face and he seems not to feel my frantic squeeze.

> B) The green wheat bends to the soft breeze. My father has kept the windows open since we left the highway. "Smell that?" he asks. "It's the smell of God's green earth."

I watch the clouds make shadow patterns on the fields and then we're turning into a driveway, past the raised flag of a mailbox, and pulling up to a white house with white sheets flapping on the clothesline. A hedge of purple blossoms, lilacs, he tells me, fill the air with pungent sweetness around the front steps. My father's hard-soled shoes clatter on the steps though my sneakers simply slide. The door flies open before I can ask to ring the bell myself.

Same place, same situation—father and child returning to the father's childhood home, but a world of difference in *mood*. The setting is both the same and not the same. What was ominous has become cheerful and promising with just a change of season, time of day, and some fresh paint.

Which of these two scenes (with their differing takes on the setting) reveals the most about the father's relationship with his parents or the child's relationship with his father? We'd have to continue with the scene to be sure, but my bet is on the gloomy winter version, because it offers the possibility that the child will see his father in a new and dimmer light, which tends to have more impact on us than a single happy moment of family conviviality.

Stephen Crane's "The Open Boat" uses setting symbolically in this tale based on his own experiences in a lifeboat after the sinking of a ship in the Spanish-American War:

Their eyes glanced level, and were fastened upon the waves that swept toward them. These waves were of the hue of slate, save for the tops, which were of foaming white … The horizon narrowed and widened, and dipped and rose, and at all times its edge was jagged with waves that seemed thrust up in points like rocks … the last effort of the grim water. There was a terrible grace in the move of the waves, and they came in silence, save for the snarling of the crests.

Crane uses his description of the setting to heighten the precarious position of these men, who, after all, are in desperate straits. But he pushes the setting, giving the sea a will, personifying it. It snarls, is grim, makes a last effort to sink these men. Moreover, the waves jut up like pointy rocks, a bit later they are described as *"barbarously* abrupt and tall." This isn't a neutral environment, it is an antagonist, and a powerful one. You might even say that the sea is a character in this classic story of man against nature. The water functions symbolically as death, trying to steal the shipwrecked men's lives.

To make setting function symbolically in a scene, the place or an aspect of it must carry a meaning beyond its factual identity and that meaning must be a part of the narrative. In other words, a crumbling castle on a moor could serve as a symbol of a disintegrating relationship but only if it plays off events or themes essential to the narrative. If, for example, the scene concerns a couple on vacation trying to hold together a failing marriage, the crumbling castle would make sense as a symbol of that marriage. On its own it is just a crumbling castle.

James Joyce, in "The Boarding House," uses setting in a scene to emphasize themes and reveal character in his story of a timid young man's entrapment in marriage to the daughter of the boardinghouse owner, Mrs. Mooney (ellipses mine):

> The belfry of George's Church sent out constant peals ... the table of the breakfast room was covered with plates on which lay yellow streaks of eggs with morsels of bacon fat ... When the table was cleared ... the sugar and butter safe under lock and key, she began to reconstruct the interview which she had had the night before with Polly ...

> ... she would have lots of time to have the matter out
> with Mr. Doran ... She was sure she would win. To begin
> with she had all the weight of social opinion on her side:
> she was an outraged mother.

It's no coincidence that the Church bells and the worshippers provide the background to this scene or that it is set on a Sunday. The strength of the church in early twentieth-century Ireland cannot be underestimated, and Mrs. Mooney, with her respectable lace curtains, will use everything in her arsenal to force young Mr. Doran, who has had an affair with Polly, to marry her, though Mrs. Mooney has, in fact, given Polly "the run of" the young men in the boardinghouse. Even the breakfast plates streaked with egg and bacon rinds can be seen as symbolic of ruin, of Polly's lost virginity. Mrs. Mooney's shrewdness is evident in her keeping her sugar and butter under lock and key and in her recycling of the bread crusts for pudding (not technically setting but behavior having to do with the setting). What seems like mere scene setting is integral information. After all, Mrs. Mooney, a butcher's daughter, "dealt with moral problems as a cleaver deals with meat ..." Mr. Doran is a goner!

Think about how the details of setting could carry more weight than simple information in one of your scenes. Do the weather, landscape, cityscape, or interior setting convey a mood? What can the details of the setting show about your character(s) in the scene? For example, what might a bedroom tell about your character? Is it messy or orderly? What pictures does she have on her dresser? Who is in those pictures and what relationship are they to her?

We've been looking at realistic settings so far but setting is just as important in surreal or fantasy works. In Philip Pullman's *The Golden Compass* we are given a detailed account of Oxford University and its holdings, and a specific description of a catacomb, before the less-than-real takes over:

> On each coffin, Lyra was interested to see, a brass plaque
> bore a picture of a different being: this one a basilisk,
> this a serpent, this a monkey. She realized that they were
> images of the dead men's daemons. As people became
> adult, their daemons lost the power to change and as-
> sumed one shape, keeping it permanently.

Pullman has grounded his fantasy in a seemingly realistic setting, and it is within that grounding that he positions the bizarre
fact of people possessing personal animal-like daemons. This is
something of a reversal of poet Marianne Moore's famous comment about writers creating "imaginary gardens with real toads
in them." Pullman has created real gardens with imaginary toads.
Either way, it is the interplay between the real and the imagined
that makes the setting function effectively within the scene.

A student once asked me how much setting is needed in re-
lation to action and dialogue. It was an impossible question to
answer in the abstract, because each scene, and each author's intention, has specific needs. But when I was writing my first novel I
made up a little mantra for myself each time I wrote a scene: "See
it, feel it." You could expand "See it" to include smell it, taste it, or
whatever other sensory details are needed, but the essence of the
mantra was that I needed to place myself inside the scene in order
to write it authentically, and to do that I would have to describe the
setting to the extent that it became real to me. Once I'd established
that setting, I needed to feel the emotions of the characters. We'll
discuss that in a minute, but to answer my student's question I'd
say you need as much setting as it takes for you and your reader
to see—and/or smell, taste, touch—the scene.

CHARACTER

Scenes reveal character through narrative description, behavior,
dialogue, and the characters' thoughts. The writer of fiction or

creative nonfiction has the benefit of internal monologue that is denied the writer of plays and movies, unless the often clunky device of the voice-over is used. Creative prose permits a writer to enter the mind of a character/narrator and dwell there, revealing to the reader what can't be observed from outside. In fiction, depending on the narrative strategy, the narrator might be omniscient, moving from one character's point of view to another, or the narration might stick to the mind of one character through close third-person or first-person point of view. In creative nonfiction, the narrator's consciousness is usually the only one the reader gets to explore from the inside, but the writer can reveal other characters in scenes by using the tools of description, behavior, and dialogue—often in combination.

REVEALING CHARACTER VIA NARRATIVE DESCRIPTION

To reveal character through description, the details you use are of utmost importance. You are in a scene; you are showing, not telling. So the details must demonstrate who that person is in order to make the scene richer and the characters more interesting. Think about all the judgments you make about people daily simply based on appearance: That man in the tattered clothes lurching down the sidewalk is homeless; this woman is dressing too young for her age; this one's a grandma; that guy in the suit, tie, and horn-rimmed glasses looks distinguished—some kind of venerable professional. We tend to make these judgments based on generalities. In your own writing, you can dress your characters so they are quickly recognizable as a jock, a preppy, homeless, etc. Or you can dig a little deeper and see if you can reveal more about the character than stereotypes. Stereotypes, like clichéd scenes, weaken your work and make it uninteresting. For instance, if the homeless guy carries a volume of Tolstoy, your reader might begin to wonder about who he was before he became homeless. If the distinguished-looking fellow is video gambling on his laptop, you might think he's in trouble. In either case, you've caught the reader's interest and made him want to know more about the character. The character has come alive for him through description—by showing, you have broken stereotypes and created reader interest.

If I write "The old lady sat on the park bench" I'm describing directly but not revealing anything about her character. But I can add to the description to individualize this old lady and give you a glimpse into her nature. I might dress her quite elegantly, with a neat, upswept coiffure, a fashionable tailored jacket, and expensive shoes with heels. From these few details you would start to get a sense of who she was. If she drew out a compact and began fussing with her lipstick, you might even think her vain, but that is moving into the realm of revealing character via behavior. We're still somewhat limited in what we can divine about this character through description alone.

REVEALING CHARACTER VIA BEHAVIOR

If I add, "The old lady drew a pile of tattered, yellowed newspaper from a tote bag and set it on her lap, then began to rip long strips from the pages," you might become more interested in the scene unfolding, which of course is any writer's intention. What is this elegantly dressed lady ripping? Is she tearing out coupons? Why would such a well-dressed lady need coupons? Is she a formerly wealthy woman fallen on hard times? But the papers are yellowed and the coupons must be long expired. Is she a papier-mâché artist? Is she crazy? There is already a tension in this scene caused by the disparity between this woman's appearance and her actions. You can use disparity between appearance and actions in your own work to increase tension and therefore reader interest. In essence you're presenting your reader with a question that needs answering—what the heck is this person doing, and why?

What could I add to this lady's behavior that would further reveal her character and add to the tension? Interaction with other characters is a great way to get the people in your story to show more of who they are. To that end, I'll put a young couple on the bench across from her so that there's the opportunity for interaction:

> The young woman was half-sitting in her boyfriend's lap, her arms around his neck and he appeared to be licking her throat. The old woman looked over and addressed them in an Austrian accent, "Excuse me. Sorry to intrude. You wouldn't happen to have a pair of scissors that you could spare, would you?"

From the above brief scene we know that the old lady is polite. She has an Austrian accent so she's foreign-born, Old World, even. And she's bonkers. We know she's out of touch with reality because it is very unlikely that these two kids just happen to have scissors on them, and it's plain weird for her to interrupt their make-out session with her request. We've just revealed more of her character via dialogue. But it isn't just the dialogue that shows who she is, it's the context in which she speaks—the inappropriateness of her dialogue, in this case. Study how your character's speech fits the setting and the events around her; if there is a disconnect between the two, you've just shown your reader something important about your character. If the speech fits the context, there are still many different character qualities you can show us about the speaker. If the old lady scolded the kids for making out in public, we'd know that she was proper or a prude. If she said something salacious, we'd think her rather outrageous and bawdy. It's your decision—once you establish your intention for your characters, their words must be chosen to further that intention.

REVEALING CHARACTER VIA INTERNAL MONOLOGUE

So far we've been talking about externals—behavior and speech. But if we want to learn what's going on inside a character, and if we're fiction writers, we can reveal her thoughts via internal monologue as she observes the young couple making out:

> Gustav used to adore my neck. I had a lovely neck. Now it's as wrinkled as the stockings on my legs. It's impossible to find hosiery that flatters these days. My legs were perfect back then, everyone said so. I had the exact ratio of thigh to calf to ankle, the three hollows one aspired to. Of course we couldn't show our legs off like these children, except when we were skating. The wool skating tights were itchy but it was worth it to be so admired in our little twirling skirts. The band playing, the scrape-scrape of the ice under our blades, the couples whirling, whirling. We didn't even feel the cold.
>
> It's cold here now, but I must finish my chore. If only I had scissors I could make the cuts straighter, the edges not so ragged. Perhaps the nanny there with the perambulator might have a pair?

Internal monologue has given this character a history, a personality, and a troubling lack of facility in reading the world around her. The ability to delve into a character's interior world is fiction's gift to writers—something playwrights and screenwriters can't do and memoirists and personal essayists can only do for their narrator. If you're writing fiction, don't waste this opportunity to show what is beneath the surface of behavior and appearance. If you're writing creative nonfiction, make sure your narrator's inner world is on the page and that your (narrator's) thoughts are sufficiently revealing of your (narrator's) character.

It always comes back to intention—knowing what you want to accomplish in your scene, then shaping your character's thoughts (or choosing your narrator's, in nonfiction) so they show what you want them to.

IN COMBINATION

Interior thoughts, actions, and dialogue don't have to work in isolation to reveal character. You can combine these elements effectively. This example from Victoria Redel's novel *Loverboy* quickly establishes the narrator's character through the interplay of dialogue and internal monologue in a scene in which the mother tries to entice her child:

> "Okay, Paul, it is time to go."
>
> "Where?" he asked not even looking up from the red-and-yellow Lego school he had been building since his bath. His voice had an edge of annoyance that no longer surprised me.
>
> Really, my actual presence, I suspect, had become a disruption.
>
> "My secret," I said offhandedly, as if I really did not even care for him to know.
>
> Finally he looked up. "What?" he asked. In his voice I heard the first genuine interest in anything I had said in weeks.
>
> "What secret?" he asked. "You have a secret?" He was surprised, I could tell, at the very notion that I might have a secret.
>
> I laughed. "How much would you like to know?"
>
> "Whatever," he said turning back to the lopsided staircase he was building.
>
> "Paul," I said. "Paul, we are going now."
>
> "In a second," he snapped.

"Loverboy," I said quietly, "would you like to drive?"

Now, just like that, he was up and rubbing close to me, saying, "Really, Mom? I can drive! But I can't really drive, Mom, you know that, right?"

We know from this excerpt that this mother will resort to extremes in order to get her young child's attention and that the child, young as he is, seems a bit worried about his mother's grasp of things. We also know that she feels rejected by her child whose interest in Lego supersedes his interest in her until she offers to let him drive. We don't know just how desperate the situation is until a bit further on in the scene when the mother expresses her distress that her son is playing with his bloody loose tooth, not because she's afraid he'll hurt himself but because the loss of a baby tooth is a sign that he is growing up, growing further from her tight clasp.

Of his Lego construction, she observes:

And now he was building that school with its little blondie teacher, his slim-hipped, impossibly earnest Miss Silken. Silky Silken. And the others. The good-watchdog secretary, Mrs. Pomeroy and the ever-helpful Principal—don't forget, children, that is principal, P-A-L.

"Loverboy," I said, "come on, let me help you build. We shall build together."

"Mom, you're not allowed in my school anymore. And I told you, call me Paul."

So there were no more chances. It would not help to snap at him, "That does not look a thing like your school. And say, *it is*, not *it's.*"

The mother's internal monologue exposes her jealousy of her son's teacher and resentment of the school officials. But it is the son's innocent line of dialogue about his mother not being allowed in his school anymore that gets us really worried for this mother and child. She is trouble—perhaps even dangerous if she is no longer allowed in the school and if, in fact, she lets her son drive in order to seduce him into obeying her wishes. Though neither of these excerpts employs behavior as a means of revelation, dialogue and internal monologue have combined to effectively illustrate a character who may be seriously disturbed. Later on in the novel, it is the mother's endangering *behavior* that reveals the full extent of her madness.

You can use the interplay between interior thoughts, dialogue, and behavior to establish and reveal character in your own scenes by deciding what you need to show your reader about the character in that particular scene. This means articulating for yourself a purpose for the scene and a purpose for the character in that scene—what your character wants in the scene and what your character will encounter by way of obstacles to that desire (or aid in fulfilling that desire). Then think of all the ways you can show that desire—through gesture, speech, inner thoughts—and discard any that seem too familiar or expected—stereotypical or clichéd. Remember not to repeat in dialogue what your character has thought internally and vice versa—once is enough. Ask yourself if these behaviors and thoughts, spoken or otherwise, are *true to your character*, not something you've just donated to them to get them through the scene. Do you want to implement a contradiction between what the character says and what the character wants? If so, let the dialogue conflict with the interior thoughts. Your reader has access to both and will know all the more about who this person really is. But you will have created tension in the scene between what is said and what is thought, and tension is very helpful in making a scene vibrant. The same goes for a disconnect between what a character says and what he does—that too adds tension. But if the disconnect is too great—if the old lady on the park bench primly powders her nose and then announces to the lovers across from her that she likes to get action too—your reader will think the character is certifiable or that the writer's conception of the character is schizophrenic. Contradiction is a useful tool but one that must be wielded carefully.

MORE ON DIALOGUE

Dialogue is just people talking, right? Wrong. Eavesdrop on strangers talking in the booth behind you in a coffee shop and compare that to a page of dialogue in a story or memoir. How often in your eavesdropping did you hear audible pauses and verbal tics—ums, errs, you knows, I means, and so forth? How often did people interrupt each other, start new topics, fail to finish a sentence? Selection and artful shaping of dialogue distinguishes it from real speech. Moreover, dialogue has a lot of work to do in a prose piece; it should never just be there to give "color."

As we just saw, dialogue can function as a means of revealing character in scenes. It can also tip off the reader to identifying characteristics such as region of origin, social class, education level, mood of speaker, whether or not someone's been drinking, etc. Dialogue can expose themes, heighten the drama, provide background, and occasionally add humor. It should do more than just one of these in a scene.

In Flannery O'Connor's story "A Good Man Is Hard to Find," the characters quickly identify themselves by their speech patterns. The wife of a diner owner, Red Sammy, speaks first:

> "It isn't a soul in this green world of God's that you can trust," she said. "And I don't count nobody out of that, not nobody," she repeated, looking at Red Sammy.
>
> "Did you hear about that criminal, The Misfit, that's escaped?" asked the grandmother.

"I wouldn't be a bit surprised if he didn't attact this place right here," said the woman. "If he hears about it being here, I wouldn't be none surprised to see him. If he hears it's two cent in the cash register, I wouldn't be a tall surprised if he..."

"That'll do," Red Sam said.

From this snippet of story, it's clear that the diner owner's wife is suspicious, loquacious, and under the thumb of her husband, Red Sammy, whom she resents and mistrusts. Her mispronunciation and idiom identify her as uneducated and countrified. She's also naïve—it isn't likely that The Misfit would make a special trip for the cash register of that "broken-down place" (as one of the family's kids refers to it a page earlier). Although the grandmother only speaks one line in this excerpt, she speaks more grammatically and is therefore likely more educated than Red Sammy's wife. The dialogue also serves to foreshadow action to follow, when the unfortunate family does, in fact, meet up with The Misfit. So the dialogue here is doing a lot of work for the story and it's also amusing.

Although the dialogue above is colorful, it's pulling a lot of other weight. Think of how you might make your own dialogue do more for your scene than just voicing a character's thoughts aloud. Do your characters speak with a regional idiom? Is there any way that their choice of words could tell your reader where they come from geographically or economically? Can you tell the mood of your characters from the manner in which they speak? How might you infuse your dialogue so it echoes themes in your piece, as the diner owner's wife does above when she discusses mistrusting people in the excerpt above? This is tricky, because you don't want your characters to become obvious mouthpieces for themes—stick figures that announce the writer's ideas—or too openly foreshadow future events so all mystery is lost. You don't want to be cueing the dramatic theme music in the background when they speak. The dialogue must always sound believable—it must seem as though it is generated naturally from the events transpiring, even though you are selecting and shaping it to your own ends. Most important: Read your dialogue aloud as you work to see if it sounds convincing. Better yet, if you can, have someone read it aloud to you.

In Janet Peery's story "Whitewing," dialogue does double and triple duty. The narrator is a fifteen-year-old boy in rural Texas, disturbed by his unconventional, widowed mother's friendship with a Salvadoran refugee—a man who will eventually become her husband. The dialogue below begins with the son's complaining about the Salvadoran, asserting that he was stupid when the mother explained the Salvadoran was here for refuge, having supported the wrong political figure. The son says:

> "How do you think this makes me look? Don't you think people are going to start talking?"
>
> She laughed. "This place," she said, "this place. And what do you suppose they'll say that they haven't said a thousand times?"
>
> I set my glass down. "That you're breaking the law."
>
> ... She sighed. "I can't imagine what your father would think of the way you're behaving."
>
> Her words struck me like a punch, and I felt sick. "Daddy wouldn't have let any wetback kiss his hand." I turned to leave. "Or his butt."

The son's ugly racism is clearly learned behavior, as his mother points out when she says "this place" and elsewhere blames his friends, carrying one of the themes of the story. Other themes—the boy's loss of his father and his oedipal as well as racist resentment of the Salvadoran—are emphasized in the dialogue. It also carries a bit of background—from the mother's words we know that the boy's dead father was more liberal than the son's friends, no matter what the boy imagines in his parting shot. Two pages later, the drama is heightened and the themes are underscored further when the mother comments "... someday perhaps you will learn compassion."

Dialogue can be used for giving background but it should not be used *primarily* for exposition. When an author forces characters to fill in via speech instead of using narrative summary, the dialogue often sounds stilted, reminiscent of those old-fashioned plays in which the butler and the maid stand in front of the audience and give exposition in the guise of conversation: "Well, after the valet saw Lady Marston slipping into the duke's bedroom, the duchess ..."

When background is carried through dialogue there has to be a reason for that background to be revealed *in the scene*. It has to have a function in the scene and there needs to be a reason that the character is telling that history *now*. If expository dialogue serves no purpose in the scene besides exposition, it is usually better to present the background through narrative summary, which will be discussed in Section II.

As for letting your dialogue carry themes, that too is tricky as once again you don't want your character to announce the meaning of the story too directly—whenever characters serve as mouthpieces for the author their believability dwindles. If the mother in the above excerpt had said, "Your father would not approve of your racism; your father would have wanted you to respect all humans but we raised you in a backward, provincial place in which you've been influenced by narrow-minded people ... ," the dialogue would have felt very stilted. Moreover, the character would have come across as though she were serving as a stand-in for the writer who was preaching to her readers. No one reads stories to be preached at.

Dialogue must be believable and appear to grow naturally from the events of the story or essay. What makes dialogue believable? First of all, people rarely make the kinds of speeches you hear in overly earnest or sentimental movies; people rarely make speeches at all in conversation. If your characters are going on at length and especially if they are using abstractions such as *courage* and *honor* or *devotion*, watch out! Second, it's not enough that your characters speak in a natural manner in general, it must be natural to them as *individuals*—what would she say at that moment, in that circumstance? Who but David Sedaris, working as an elf for a department store in his essay "Santaland Diaries," would say (or, in this case, sign) to customers waiting to see Santa, "SANTA HAS A TUMOR IN HIS HEAD THE SIZE OF AN OLIVE. MAYBE IT WILL GO AWAY TOMORROW BUT I DON'T THINK SO."

Ask yourself, as you look over your dialogue, what it's doing for the scene? Does it move the scene forward, heighten tension, put forth themes, reveal character? When you read it aloud to see how it sounds, check for words or lines that could be cut. Is it believable? If not, why not?

For more on natural and stilted dialogue, see "The Sins of Scenes" (page 87).

A Note On Dialect

Dialect can offend. In the past, dialect was often used for derogatory ethnic stereotyping, as with the minstrel-like portrayal of African-Americans such as Mammy in *Gone With the Wind,* who says, "Ef you doan care 'bout how folks talks 'bout dis fambly, Ah does … " or the Jewish mobster Meyer Wolfsheim in *The Great Gatsby* who talks about making "gonnections." Contemporary writers should be very wary about employing dialect. There are some authors who insist that dialect should never be used and that a writer must establish characters' speech habits through the use of word choice and rhythm. Others believe that the richness of American English derives in part from those whose speech deviates from "standard" English; words like *klutz* and *schmuck* or *'hood* and *homeboy* have been incorporated into the lexicon and should be used in speech. Still others believe that only members of a particular ethnic group have the right to make use of their group's speech patterns. Ultimately you must make your own decision about your writing, but at the least you should ask yourself if you are using stereotypes and therefore diminishing the humanity of any character, which will only weaken the work in the end.

A Few Suggestions for Dialogue Tags, Adverbs, and Verbs of Speech

- Dialogue tags are essential unless you are able to show through the actions and description who is speaking. It's very frustrating when a reader has to read back to see who is talking when.

- Be very sparing with adverbs following the tag. The action and words should show the manner in which the character is speaking. You don't need "Drop dead!" she said *angrily,* since the dialogue shows her anger.

- Make sure your dialogue tag is actually a verb of speech. "You're cute," she *winked* makes no sense.

- Avoid overly colorful verbs of speech. There's nothing wrong with good old *said* or *says.* Pointed or whimsical verbs of speech tend can distract from the dialogue as in "Get out!" she *raged,* or "Can't you kids quit bothering that cat?" the old lady *harrumphed.*

Finally, if you don't know how to punctuate dialogue, look at the dialogue in any reputable book. Or take note: "I get so aggravated by incorrect dialogue punctuation," the editor said, "I throw those manuscripts right out."

POINT OF VIEW

Most memoirs and other forms of creative nonfiction, except for a few rare cases, are written in the first person. With fiction, the traditional point of view choices are first-person or third-person narration, either omniscient or close, with the uncommon use of the second person. Let's return for a moment to the paragraph about Margaret and the dentist from the introduction.

> Pinned to the reclining dentist chair with her mouth stretched into the shape of a silent scream, Margaret realized, even before the Novocain took hold, that Dr. Verbsky would make the perfect father for her yet-to-be-conceived child.

It wouldn't be terribly difficult to recast this in first person, nor would it make an enormous change in effect because the third-person narration above is *close* third, meaning it stays within the perceptions of a single mind:

> Pinned to the reclining dentist chair with my mouth stretched into the shape of a silent scream, I realized, even before the Novocain took hold, that Dr. Verbsky would make the perfect father for my yet-to-be-conceived child.

Although the first person makes us feel a little closer to the narrator (who is speaking to us, after all), the same conflicts remain as in the close third-person version. If we recast it in omniscient third person we can move to the perceptions of other characters, Dr. Verbsky in this case:

> Dr. Verbsky picked up the explorer from the papered
> tray and peered inside Margaret's mouth. Not good, he
> thought, though it wasn't his patient's gums or her molars
> he was considering. It was the tingle in his left arm and
> hand that could be repetitive motion injury or it *could* be
> the harbinger of a heart attack. His cholesterol had been
> climbing ... "Open wider, please," he instructed.

Once we have the option of seeing into Dr. Verbsky's mind
we are offered a whole new conflict that Margaret hasn't even
imagined—Dr. Verbsky's real or neurotic health worries—and
we have the added tension of the disconnect between Margaret's and Verbsky's thoughts.

If we shift the point of view to second person, the effect is
altogether different:

> Pinned to the reclining dentist chair with your mouth
> stretched into the shape of a silent scream, you realize,
> even before the Novocain takes hold, that Dr. Verb-
> sky would make the perfect father for your yet-to-be-
> conceived child.

You can use second-person point of view to accomplish two
things: (1) It puts the reader in the position of being the primary character "you", or (2) alternatively, it creates a sense that
the narrator is detached from himself, alienated, estranged.
This worked very effectively in *Bright Lights, Big City,* Jay
McInerney's novel of a young man lost in the cocaine culture
of yuppie New York in the 1980s who has become a stranger
to himself. No matter what is happening in the scene, the second-person point of view adds conflict due to the tension that
underlies the question of why am I, the reader, being forced to
be the main character, or why is this narrator so disconnected
from himself?

You might notice that I changed the tense in this last version of the Margaret and Verbsky scene, from past to present. Why? It's not a rule, just a personal preference. There's something about the second person that seems to call for the immediacy and staccato nature of present tense *in this paragraph.*

How then do you decide which point of view to employ in a scene, let alone a book? If the narrative voice and point of view don't come to you naturally, it's worth trying different versions to see which works best according to your intention for the scene. To complicate the issue, even a single first-person narrator can have various voices within a scene. There can be the voice of the narrator at an earlier and a later stage in his life. It is more common to come across the retrospective voice in reflective summary, but an older, wiser, or at least more articulate narrator can appear in scenes as well, as in the excerpt from Bernard Cooper's essay "Burl's" in the chapter on "Time" when he refers to himself as "an incredulous child stalled in their path," surely not the language of an eight-year-old.

How do you choose whether or not to use the voice of limited awareness, or the retrospective voice, in fiction or creative nonfiction scenes? The limited voice has immediacy; an older and/or wiser voice can interpret and comprehend even in the middle of the ongoing action. You must weigh which effect is desired. Often writers will try different versions, comparing the success of each. Sometimes both voices will appear in a single scene, as in Cooper's essay "Burl's."

MOVEMENT—CHANGE OVER TIME

Movement in scenes exists on multiple levels. Movement can be literal—through space as in actions, gestures, locomotion—but there is the larger form of movement: When you get to the end of the scene, just as when you get to the end of a book, you want to feel that you are in a different place than when you entered.

Within that scene something has changed, or something has changed in your perception of the narrator or characters. It's a form of psychic or emotional movement.

Return to the Amy Tan excerpt on page 14. The physical movement in the scene plays out with the mother entering the room, insisting the daughter practice piano. The daughter resists. The mother yanks her by the arm, snaps off the television, and places her on the piano bench. At that point the physical movement within the story is finished. But the psychological movement continues. The mother tells the girl that there are only two kinds of daughters, obedient and disobedient. The daughter attacks in return, telling her mother she wishes she weren't her daughter. The daughter feels both horror and elation at expressing her real feelings. The mother fights back , saying "Too late." This is the end of the excerpt I used, but the scene continues. The daughter, wanting to push her mother further, takes her best shot: "I wish I were dead! Like them." She's referring to her mother's first daughters, left behind in China, something the family doesn't talk about. At this, the mother crumbles and backs out of the room, as if "blowing away like a small brown leaf, thin, brittle, lifeless."

The *physical* movement of the scene begins with the mother entering the room and ends with her exiting it. The *emotional* movement of the scene contains the struggle of wills between mother and daughter, the daughter's forceful attempt at autonomy including her cruel reference, and the mother's giving up, stunned. Although the scene ends at this point, the reader can infer that the daughter will be left with a potent mix of emotions—a new sense of power, shame at her own cruelty, and wonder at her mother's surprising vulnerability. This is truly a turning point scene. The emotional movement is far more complex than the physical movement of the scene. Yet both are necessary and both require a kind of logic.

Examine the movement within your own scenes and see if you can distinguish physical and/or emotional movement. Is the emotional movement in your scene within a character (has anyone changed over the course of the scene) or is the emotional movement supposed to occur within the reader, who has a new perception of the character(s) and their situations?

Physical *and* emotional movement are not necessary in every scene. A scene might take place in a short time period in which no one moves from her chair. But if no emotional movement occurs in that scene of two people in their chairs, such as some kind of revealing interaction, or if the reader's perception of those people doesn't change over the course of the scene, the scene would feel pretty static. It could hardly be considered vibrant. That said, not all scenes need to be highly dramatic, like the scene between the girl and her mother in Amy Tan's novel, to show movement.

Let's look at another example, this time less dramatic, though entertaining, and still showing movement, from Bill Bryson's memoir of walking the Appalachian Trail, *A Walk in the Woods*. In this scene, early into his hike, Bryson and his trail partner Katz encounter a fellow traveler, Mary Ellen (ellipses mine):

"So what are you guys eating?" she said, plonking herself down on a spare log ..."Noodles? Big mistake. Noodles have got like no energy. I mean like zero." She unblocked her ears. (Bryson has already described this violent and loud activity involving pinching her nose and blowing out.) "Is that a Starship tent?"

I looked at my tent. "I don't know."

"Big mistake. They must have seen you coming at the camping store. What did you pay for it?"

"I don't know."

"Too much. That's how much. You should have gotten a three-season tent."

"It is a three-season tent."

"Pardon me saying so, but it is like seriously dumb to come out here in March without a three-season tent."

"It is a three-season tent."

"You're lucky you haven't froze yet. You should go back and like punch out the guy that sold it to you because he's been like, you know, negligible selling you that."

"Believe me, it is a three-season tent."

She ... shook her head impatiently. "*That's* a three-season tent." She indicated Katz's tent.

"That's exactly the same tent."

"Whatever. How many miles did you do today?"

"About ten." Actually we had done eight point four ...

"Ten miles? Is that all? You guys must be like really out of shape. I did fourteen-two."

"How many have your lips done?" said Katz, looking up from his noodles.

She fixed him with one of her more severe squints. "Same as the rest of me, of course." She cleared her ears. "I started at Gooch Gap."

"So did we. That's only eight point four miles."

She shook her head sharply, as if shooing a particularly tenacious fly. "Fourteen-two."

"No, really, it's only eight point four."

"Excuse me, but I just *walked* it. I think I ought to know." And then suddenly: "God, are those Timberland boots? *Mega* mistake. How much did you pay for them?"

What is the movement in this scene? A stranger enters and we get an increasingly clearer picture of her obnoxiousness and Bryson and Katz's growing annoyance as the scene evolves. Katz is eventually spurred to make a sarcastic comment, which goes right over her head. We come to see that she has a poor grasp of language—she says *negligible* when she means *negligent*.

She is bull-headed and critical—of their equipment, their fitness, their use of their money—and can't be deterred from her insistence on her superior abilities in the face of facts. She's a comical character and serves to show the reader that Bryson and Katz aren't the least prepared of all through-hikers on the Appalachian Trail. We also learn that they are fairly tolerant men since they don't strangle Mary Ellen and leave her on the side of the path. Granted, the emotional and physical movement of the scene are fairly negligible, to use Mary Ellen's word. But there *is* movement here; we understand by the end of the scene what we didn't know the minute Mary Ellen appeared—these hikers are vulnerable to more than just blisters and wild animals on their journey—other hikers can be, if not scary, then crazy-making. The level of movement is appropriate to this scene, just as the level of movement was in the Amy Tan scene. The movement in your scenes must be suited to the material. You don't want people jumping out of their seats and running in and out of the building if the scene is one of a character's crisis of faith during a church service (unless the church is on fire).

There is another kind of movement I haven't yet discussed—chronology, or the arrangement of actions or material in the scene. Imagine some of the scenes we've discussed rearranged, for example, the scene of the teenager dying after running through a sliding glass door in the excerpt from Michael Cunningham's novel *A Home at the End of the World*. If the author had begun the scene with Carlton's death, then stepped back to show how it happened step by step, the impact would be greatly lessened, for the reader is hoping all the way through that Carlton won't senselessly die.

If Mrs. Mooney, in Joyce's story "The Boardinghouse," had it out with Mr. Doran first, then sat down to watch the maid lock up the butter and save the crusts, what would change? You wouldn't have as full a sense of Mrs. Mooney as a character and might not understand her strategizing.

Generally, authors rearrange chronology *among different scenes*—perhaps putting an adult scene before a childhood scene—rather than rearranging chronology *within* a single scene. I recently read a very good student story in which the whole is told in reverse including some events within scenes. But this device has a purpose in the story, which is playing with memory and time. Telling stories backwards has been done before; Charles Baxter's novel *First Light* is told backwards. And even the Fitzgerald story "The Curious Case of Benjamin Button," uses a version of this device, having the main character be born old and grow young, though the story still follows a normal chronology, even if the character doesn't.

In any case, when an author chooses to rearrange the chronology *of a scene* with flashbacks or taking events out of order, there should be an important reason for that choice. It must serve the piece more than it disrupts. And remember, it *is* a device, and if not used with great delicacy and skill, the device can distract from the scene's impact.

DETAIL

I discussed the use of detail in the section on setting, but detail, of course, can go beyond setting. What is the role of detail in scene? At their best, details do more than just create a believable world in which the story or essay or chapter exists. Details can also carry themes, reveal character, heighten or provide drama. A mystery story might completely turn on a detail such as a missing murder weapon. The same can be true of a literary piece, as in one scene in Susan Minot's novel *Monkeys* when the family is on an outing, happy because the alcoholic father isn't drinking, and then they hear the hiss of a snapped beer can top. That small but explosive detail turns the mood from pleasant hopefulness to gloomy frustration.

First, let's distinguish between ordinary concrete details such as a brown dog, a ceramic cup, a hose on the lawn, the building on the left—and details that carry greater meaning. All of the details mentioned above could be significant in a particular scene. If seeing a brown dog reminds a character of the time her father ran over her beloved pet, a brown dog is significant in that scene. If a smashed ceramic cup signals the end of a relationship, the cup bears weight. If the sight of a coiled hose (as in Andre Dubus's story "The Doctor") makes a physician realize he might have been able to save a drowning child trapped in a stream by a chunk of fallen cement, the hose carries tremendous importance and may haunt him for a long time. In other words, details become significant when the writer assigns weight to them, allowing them to reverberate within a scene.

Notice the use of concrete and weighty details in this excerpt taken from the chapter "The World's Greatest Fisherman" in the novel *Love Medicine* by Louise Erdrich:

> The morning before Easter Sunday, June Kashpaw was walking down the clogged main street of oil boomtown Williston, North Dakota, killing time before the noon bus arrived that would take her home. She was a long-legged Chippewa woman, aged hard in every way except how she moved. Probably it was the way she moved, easy as a young girl on slim hard legs, that caught the eye of the man who rapped at her from inside the window of the Rigger Bar ...
>
> ... Even through the watery glass she could see that he wasn't all that old and that his chest was thickly padded in dark red nylon and expensive down.
>
> There were cartons of colored eggs on the bar, each glowing like a jewel in its wad of cellophane. He was peeling one, sky blue as a robin's, palming it while he

thumbed the peel aside, when she walked through the door. Although the day was overcast, the snow itself reflected such light that she was momentarily blinded. It was like going underwater. What she walked toward more than anything else was that blue egg in the white hand, a beacon in the murky air.

He ordered a beer for her, a Blue Ribbon, saying she deserved a prize for being the best thing he'd seen for days. He peeled an egg for her, a pink one, saying it matched her turtleneck. She told him it was no turtleneck. You called these things shells. He said he would peel that for her too, if she wanted, then he grinned at the bartender and handed her the naked egg.

We quickly learn from the description *expensive down* that June Kashpaw has little money of her own, little enough to note the value of a down vest, which is furthered by the fact that she must ride the bus and seems to have no car. She is described as being *aged hard* except in how she moves. She's a woman who has lived through a lot though she retains something youthful, perhaps innocent, about her. The beer isn't just a beer but a *Blue Ribbon*, setting us up for the oil rigger's come-on line. June insists her jersey isn't a *turtleneck*, which carries with it the association of an animal with protection and a hard carapace, but a *shell*, like the shells on the eggs the rigger peels, fragile and removable. The rigger grins at the bartender, not at June. It's a small gesture but one that reveals June's further vulnerability—she is being made sport of, the focus of leering men. Additional details: The bar is dark and June is blinded, the eggs are a beacon. Williston is an oil boomtown, and like most boomtowns it will have its day and be left behind as oil runs out and the opportunists move on, just as this rigger will use June and move on. It is the morning before Easter Sunday, and as the story continues the symbolic associations with death and resurrection will play out as well.

Most remarkable to me when reading this story is that every detail is both concrete *and* significant, so the highly symbolic nature of Erdrich's prose never overwhelms the story being told. It is always grounded, always believable. It is a measure of Erdrich's artistry that this piece works on so many levels.

Few of us could use *so many* significant and symbolic details in a single scene without seeming heavy-handed. But the inclusion of significant details is important in making the work richly layered and meaningful as well as vibrant.

The details in a first-person narrative, be it fiction or nonfiction, automatically reveal the character of the narrator because the first-person narrator has made the choice to notice and select those details that have meaning to him. The following excerpt comes from Sue William Silverman's essay "The Pat Boone Fan Club" (ellipses mine).

> Slowly I scanned the [magnifying] glass across black-and-white photographs of Pat Boone in the latest issue of *Life* magazine. In one, he, his wife, Shirley, and four daughters perch on a tandem bicycle in front of their New Jersey home, not many miles from my own. I was particularly drawn to the whiteness of the photos. Pat Boone's white-white teeth beamed at me, his white bucks spotless ... I traced my finger across his magnified image ... in the photograph all movement was frozen, the bicycle wheels stationary, never to speed away from me ... It was this crisp, clean, unchanging certainty that I craved.

The intensity of the narrator's attention to detail is striking in this excerpt. She is obsessively seeking something abstract in the details frozen in the photograph: a safe family that can't "speed away" from her. Pat Boone's whiteness—his "white-white" teeth and "spotless white bucks" hold symbolic weight, a purity that the narrator, through no fault of her own, has lost.

The details provide the illusion of a "crisp, clean, unchanging certainty" that she craves. Even without that final line of reflection, offered from an older, wiser perspective, the reader gets a strong sense of this troubled teenaged girl based on her attention to specific details.

For those of you writing memoir or personal essays, be aware that the details you include always reveal what's important to your narrative persona, and they go a long way toward setting the mood and hinting at themes. If you, as narrator, choose to describe the tilted, broken, lichen-covered gravestones in a forgotten cemetery rather than the narrow white birches reaching skyward as you walk a New England country lane, your reader will focus on intimations of death rather than on images of natural beauty. Being aware of your intention will inform the choices you make in selection of details.

LANGUAGE

Attention to language is essential in making scenes vibrant. By language, I mean syntax, diction, imagery, metaphor, similes, and dialogue, the last of which we've already discussed. Syntax refers to sentence structure, diction to wording. If all of your sentences are simple subject/verb/object constructions (*He opened the door. He picked up the newspaper.*) your reader will soon grow tired of the repetitive structure and probably believe that the character being described is some kind of somnambulist, moving in a waking dream. I can imagine situations in which this sort of simple structural repetition would be appropriate—perhaps if a character is in shock, or emotionally shut down, or, as in Cormac McCarthy's chilling post-apocalyptic novel *The Road*, living within a hopeless nightmare. McCarthy, however, alternates such simple constructions with longer, complex, compound sentences. The simple structure, if carried out for too long without deviation, risks numbing readers while portraying a numb character. On the other hand, extremely long, convoluted sentences can leave a reader gasping for a chance to take a mental breath. Again, there are always exceptions to the rule, and there are very powerful writers such as Faulkner who have used such complicated syntax and long sentences to great effect. Generally, however, varied syntax and sentence length add to the liveliness of the prose.

Diction—word choice—can set the tone of a piece as in this excerpt from Sandra Cisneros's novel *The House on Mango Street*. The narration here reflects the voice of a child:

> If you give me five dollars I will be your friend forever.
> That's what the little one tells me.
> Five dollars is cheap since I don't have any friends except Cathy who is only my friend till Tuesday.
> Five dollars, five dollars.
> She is trying to get somebody to chip in so they can buy a bicycle from this kid named Tito. They already have ten dollars and all they need is five more.
> Don't talk to them, says Cathy. Can't you see they smell like a broom.
> But I like them. Their clothes are crooked and old. They are wearing shiny Sunday shoes without socks. It makes their bald ankles all red, but I like them. Especially the big one who laughs with all her teeth.

Notice the word choices. To capture the child's voice in this scene, Cisneros's narrator uses *till* instead of *until*. Her "friend only till Tuesday" (another childlike locution), Cathy, says that the other kids "smell like a broom," not an adult observation. And the narrator's descriptions are childlike as well—"shiny Sunday shoes," "bald ankles," "laughs with all her teeth."

If you want your narrator to sound like a child, you must not only choose the words a child would use but the details that a child would observe. If you're reaching for an adult but informal, conversational tone, you'd choose words that an adult would use in normal conversation, such as Raymond Carver's narrator in the story "Cathedral"—"This blind man, an old friend of my wife's, he was on his way to spend the night." Notice that Carver puts in the grammatically incorrect and unnecessary word "he" ten words in. It's in there not for clarification but to create a conversational tone.

If, in contrast to Carver's narrator, you want your narrator to sound educated and erudite, you might use language similar to that of Colin Thubron in his travel narrative *Where Nights Are Longest*. Here the diction displays the narrator's response to a city in Soviet Russia:

> We wandered towards the Park of Culture where a monument commemorated the defenders of Smolensk against Napoleon. It was ringed by the graves of early Bolshevik leaders, but Ivan dismissed them. "They're not important. I don't know who they are." At the park entrance the city's board of honor announced the regional heads of factories and institutes who had won prizes or exceeded their output quotas. Their photographs gazed down at us with a hollow and illustrious fixity, as if responsibility had steeped them all in the same deadening brine.

Thubron's diction is less formal than eloquent, though it becomes conversational when he includes the dialogue of the people he meets. Still, he uses a number of more complex and sometimes Latinate words: commemorated, exceeded, illustrious, fixity. Thubron's attitude toward the placards praising Communist achievements is clearly reflected in his diction; the photographed faces are stiff and "hollow," as if "steeped in the same deadening brine."

Within the category of diction, verbs are particularly influ-
ential. In the section on time, I discussed the ways in which verbs
were used to speed up the action in Michael Cunningham's novel,
and how they slowed time in Bernard Cooper's essay "Burl's".
But time is only one of the elements that can be influenced by
verb choices. Take a moment to consider the emotional associations these common verbs hold for you:

cry	exhale
twist	glance
leap	waltz
scratch	yawn
jam	punch
chew	signal
ponder	negotiate
honor	melt
whisper	mediate
soothe	slap
stomp	bathe
shoot	mangle
wait	expire
yank	caress
croak	ramble

Compare *he croaked* to *he expired*. In both examples, the sub-
jects are equally dead. But each verb carries with it the narrator's
attitude toward the dead person as well as information about
the manner in which each person died. The tone is scornful vs.
respectful (or euphemistic), perhaps even harsh vs. peaceful.
Maybe a narrator who uses the verb *croak* is protecting herself
from experiencing loss, not simply being callous. The context
would help us decipher the meaning here, but the verbs certainly
set up different expectations and associations, and therefore

affect mood and tone. Your verb choices will do the same, so choose them carefully.

METAPHOR AND SIMILE

Ideally metaphors and similes make sense within the context of the scene. When I was a young writer I argued fiercely and uselessly with a teacher that I could compare southern New Hampshire urban sprawl to kudzu clogging a forest. The teacher said the image was inappropriate for a northern New England setting, as kudzu is a species that has invaded the South. I was wrong; the teacher was right. There wasn't any logic to my simile beyond the idea of something being clogged. You'll want to make sure that the metaphors and similes you choose fit the material that contains them.

Isaac Babel's classic story "Crossing Into Poland" contains the line "The orange sun rolled down the sky like a lopped-off head ... " With this disturbing simile, Babel sets up the themes and violent actions to come; it is 1920 and the Russian Red Army has entered and is laying waste to villages in Poland. If he'd said, "the orange sun looked like a child's bright balloon," he would have missed the chance to advance his themes.

Sometimes an author might create a comparison that is intentionally jarring, making use of oppositions, as when Babel, in his Red Cavalry stories, describes machine guns " ... dragged up onto the hill like calves on halters ... They moved up side by side, like a well-ordered herd, clanking reassuringly. The sun played on their dusty muzzles. I saw a rainbow on their steel." Babel's imagery emphasizes the brutal absurdity of the engines of war invading a peaceful, pastoral setting. Here are a few more striking Babel similes:

"Sounds scraped out of my violin like iron filings."

"The sun soared up into the sky and spun like a red bowl on the tip of a spear."

"The stars scattered in front of the window like urinating soldiers."

"In the room next door, the butcher and his wife, in the grip of love, thrashed about like two large fish trapped in a jar ... "

In comparison to Isaac Babel's unique imagery, clichéd language has no impact other than to make a reader turn away. No matter how exciting the action in a scene might be, tired, overused language will flatten and kill it. When eyes *sparkle* or *twinkle*, when hair is *jet black* or a man loves his girlfriend *more than life itself*, we know we are in the hands of a lazy or inexperienced writer who hasn't taken the time to find fresh language. The writer has not earned the right to keep us reading. If you want your scenes to be vibrant your language must be too. That's not to say you should hype up language to the point of absurdity so the diction and imagery distract from the scene. But, in the act of composition and revision, work to keep your language fresh.

Chapter 5

THE SINS OF SCENES

THE SIN OF THE BAD HEMINGWAY/ CARVER (TAKE YOUR PICK) IMITATION

When I was a graduate student in an MFA program and then later, when I taught undergraduate fiction writing, quite a few young, usually male, students were enamored of Hemingway. Their male characters were close-mouthed or terse when they had to speak; neither they nor the readers had much access to their emotions. They showed grace under pressure and took action when necessary. They were wounded by life but very brave. They wrote a lot of sentences using *was* and *were*, as in, *the malls were very large but we didn't go to them anymore.* Soon these young writers became enamored of Raymond Carver and started writing stories with imitative titles like "What We Talk About When We Talk About Sex" or "Will You Please Roll Over Please." The moral of the story is, write your own story.

Of course, emulation of great writers can be a good way to learn craft. You can analyze how their scenes are built and discover how they show rather than tell in their scenes. But in the end, writers have to find their own voices and their own styles and put them to use in their own work. Some writers have such distinct voices and such unique visions right from the get-go that this isn't a problem for them. If this isn't true of you, and if you, like the majority of writers, have to struggle to find your own style and voice, you'll need to be on the lookout for instances in your work when you've taken on the style and mannerisms of writers you admire. Just as you wouldn't want to plagiarize directly from someone else's book, you don't want to inadvertently "steal" their voice or their story. For one thing, readers will notice the imitation and won't appreciate it. For another, you'll be cheating yourself of one of the great satisfactions of writing, which is to discover what it is you want to say and your own way to say it.

THE SIN OF STILTED DIALOGUE

Dialogue sounds false whenever it contains information that the characters would already know but the writer inserts as exposition, as in "My mother, Geraldine, would be very happy to come to your house for dinner Uncle Joseph." Obviously, the dialogue should be more along the lines of "Mom would love to come for dinner, thanks." We assume the uncle knows the speaker's mother's name already.

Dialogue also sounds stilted when characters speak outside of their own idiom. When my first novel was being copyedited in manuscript, an overzealous copy editor wanted me to change a line in which an Alaskan fisherman in a bar jokes about committing *"hari-kari."* The copy editor changed it to the correct term for Japanese ritual suicide, *hara-kiri.* I argued that my character would use the familiar Americanized version, even if it were incorrect. Had the character called it the more formal term in Japanese, *seppuku*, the dialogue would have been even more stilted.

In that instance the dialogue was being criticized inappropriately for being too informal; when the dialogue is too formal, it also becomes stilted. While a certain academic might speak in term of dialectics and discourse modalities to his advanced literary theory class, if he spoke that way to his plumber it would either be laughable or pathetic. If not being used for comic effect it would just be bad dialogue. As I noted in the dialogue chapter earlier, read your dialogue aloud. If you find yourself stumbling over the words your characters are speaking in your scenes, it's time to revise.

THE SIN OF NOTHING HAPPENS

If a narrator or character takes her car for an oil change and no important events or interactions ensue, you could and probably should just skip the scene and summarize it. "I got my oil changed in the morning before I went to the grocery and the dry cleaner's." Or leave it out. Each aspect of the day doesn't deserve a developed scene if none of these events holds particularly revealing information about the character, or advance the plot or themes of the piece. You don't need to make the reader experience, via scenes, a character's humdrum errand-filled life in order to make the point that the character's life is indeed tedious.

Of course you could write any of these events in a way that revealed character—if the narrator got into a fight with the dry cleaner or spied her ex-husband with his new girlfriend over the produce display, for instance. Assuming that nothing as exciting as all that occurs, save the scenes for more important occasions and compress time through summary.

You might use very quiet or slow scenes to set up for something to come later, but, in general, if the scene does little in terms of heightening the complications or furthering the plot or themes, consider summarizing instead.

THE SIN OF CREDIBILITY PROBLEMS

First there's the simple problem of lack of continuity, as they say in the movie business—one scene contradicting another. If you have a mother with three kids in one scene and the same mother has seven kids in the next scene and it's only six months later, there's a credibility problem (or she's done some mighty fast adopting). On a less obvious level, lack of credibility can occur in situations such as when children are preternaturally wise or always smarter than their parents, like those TV sitcom kids who talk with the ironic smarts of little Jon Stewarts or David Lettermans.

Lack of credibility is a real problem in memoirs or personal essays in which the first-person narrator, a stand-in for the author, fails to move us or fails to make readers trust and believe emotions or even facts. We've heard plenty about the controversies over falsified memoirs, such as James Frey's or JT Leroy's, but readers can find a narrator lacking in credibility due to an attitude of self-pity or self-aggrandizing; if the narrator is always the victim of others' wrongs or always wins the day, the reader is eventually going to feel resentful and distrustful. To be credible, a memoir narrator writing from an adult perspective must be self-aware.

Granted, in fiction we have the device of the unreliable narrator, as in Eudora Welty's famous story "Why I Live at the P.O.," and there are those memoirists, such as Lauren Slater, who have made a career out of unreliability, as in her book *Lying*. But these are cases in which the author deliberately invites you to mistrust the narrator. In most novels and memoirs, trust between reader and narrator is essential. Don't risk losing that trust by making your narrator either too self-regarding or too villainous to believe in your scenes.

THE SIN OF SENTIMENTAL SCENES

What is the difference between sentiment and sentimental? I think of it as the difference between real sugar and artificial sweetener. Sentimental scenes are as artificial as Sweet'N Low.

A sentimental scene tries to *manipulate* emotion from the reader, usually pity or nostalgia or warm and fuzzy feelings. Of course you want your reader to be moved by the events in your story. What you don't want to do is turn off your reader with scenes in which you attempt to squeeze out pity or nostalgia or fuzzy feelings via mushy, maudlin writing. Most modern readers don't have the tolerance for sentimentality that readers had in the days of Charles Dickens. Even before our day, Dickens's novel *The Old Curiosity Shop* inspired Oscar Wilde to say that "One must have a heart of stone to read the death of Little Nell without laughing." It's the perfect example of sentimentality backfiring.

Even today there are practitioners of the tearjerker scene, in which lovers must part with a lot of weeping or someone noble dies. Generally the sentimental death scene requires the dying person to be an angel of some sort—already artificially sweetened—or to have a deathbed conversion to goodness. Frequently last-minute forgiveness is featured. You can practically hear the harps playing. Please don't misunderstand—I'm not at all against a scene *showing emotion* or *provoking emotion* in the reader. What I'm against is fake emotion—emotion that is forced in the characters and in the reader. How can you tell the difference? When you are moved by something you read, ask yourself if the emotional intensity in the scene feels earned. Does it match the level of intensity of emotion you felt when reading? If the characters are experiencing heightened emotions but you aren't, the writer has left you out by not making those emotions convincing. The same goes for your writing. And be very careful about using such cliché and sentimental images phrasings as "a single tear ran down her cheek." What happens when you use sentimentality rather than sentiment is that even though you're creating a scene, you are still telling, not showing. You are telling your reader to feel something that you have failed to show in a convincing way. And that defeats the purpose of scenes.

Scene ⟳

Exercises:

a.) Create a brief scene in which conflict is apparent between two characters. The conflict can be small, say, over a choice of restaurant, or large, such as a divorce.

b.) Write a scene between a cop and a driver he's pulled over. Write it in present tense and then rewrite it in past tense. How do these tense shifts alter the tone of the scene? Which works better here? Why?

c.) Go to a public space and choose one detail (of appearance, gesture, voice, action) for each person you observe that reveals something important about that person. Write a scene in which details reveal character.

d.) Write a short scene in which a parent and young or adult child return to the parent's childhood home. The first time you write it make the scene occur in the winter, in the early evening. Then rewrite that scene in the morning, mid-summer. Consider the way time and setting affect the mood and tone of the two versions.

e.) Go to a public place where you can overhear but not see people nearby—a café with booths or public transportation work particularly well—and eavesdrop on a conversation. Write down as much of the dialogue as you need to establish the relationship between or among the speakers. Is there a power relationship? What is the nature of the information being passed? Is it merely chat, is someone trying to persuade, is there a conflict or does one of the speakers have an agenda? Can you individualize the speakers from their words alone?

f.) Write an animal death scene that is neither sentimental nor cliché.

g.) Write a list of ten similes that are fresh and surprising.

h.) Rewrite the parent and child scene, above, from a different point of view. If you wrote in third person, rewrite it in first person. Or change the point-of-view character from child to parent or vice versa.

Telling:
Creating Essential Summaries

*N*ow for the part that so many writers have been discouraged from engaging in: the important act of telling as well as showing. Telling, or *summary* in the craft sense, not the middle school sense, is useful and sometimes absolutely necessary for providing background; condensing time; recounting events that don't deserve a scene yet are still important to the narrative; letting us in on characters' interior lives; and offering interpretation and reflection where appropriate. Where appropriate does not mean repeating what has already been shown well in a scene; it means an opportunity for the narrator to comment on events and characters in a way that will add texture and depth to the piece. It's not a summing up but a digging deeper.

Note: Although I have separated the functions of summary (such as providing background, compression of time, etc.) for ease of examination and explanation, many of them overlap.

Chapter 6

THE USES OF SUMMARY

PROVIDING BACKGROUND

In their most basic and frequently used form, summaries provide background information. Why does a story or essay need summarized background? Sometimes, in order to fully understand characters' actions and emotions or the unfolding of events, we need information that doesn't arise naturally within a scene. We may need to know characters' personal or family history in order to understand them. Stuffing that kind of information into scenes by means of dialogue or characters thinking about past events in the midst of ongoing action can be clunky. Also, we might not know what attitude to take toward what is happening in a scene if we don't have the context, but trying to create myriad scenes to show the context for everything will simply take up too much space and slow the action. Background summary can provide your reader with information that the characters might not even know, and this gap between reader knowledge and character ignorance can add tension and even suspense.

For example, if we don't know via background summary that the waters off the coast of a vacation spot have had a recent influx of sharks, we won't know to be scared when the family heads for the water. If we had a scene in which someone warned them, we'd think the family foolhardy rather than innocent as they begin splashing around. Yes, you could add a scene in which fishermen notice the sharks, but if your story is about the family rather than about sharks, do you really want to take up space with fishermen scenes? That kind of quickie establishing scene is better suited to the movies than to prose.

An example of using background summary to fill in a character's history appears in F. Scott Fitzgerald's *The Great Gatsby*:

> My family have been prominent, well-to-do people in this middle-western city for three generations. The Carraways are something of a clan and we have a tradition that we're descended from the Dukes of Buccleuch, but the actual founder of my line was grandfather's brother who came here in fifty-one, sent a substitute to the Civil War and started the wholesale hardware business that my father carries on to this day.

This summary would sound ridiculous if spoken as dialogue, and it would feel forced if stuffed into a character's thoughts in the midst of a scene, but as summary it smoothly gives us important information about our narrator, Nick Carraway.

A warning: Background summary stops the flow of ongoing narrative just as flashbacks slow down scenes. Therefore you have to have good reasons for including it. It has to be doing heavy lifting for you; all the better if it does more than one thing.

MAKING BACKGROUND SUMMARY DO DOUBLE DUTY

The above Fitzgerald excerpt, which occurs early in the novel, serves more purpose than just giving us Nick Carraway's family history. In this summary we learn that Nick Carraway's family was full of pretensions, self-inventors, and liars, topics that the novel will develop as it goes on to describe Jay Gatsby's self-invented life. The author has used summary here to provide background and to set up important themes.

You can use background summary to provide necessary information *and* to carry themes, set up expectations, develop suspense, or even to get a story going once you fully articulate, to yourself, your intentions for the piece. In other words, Fitzgerald knew he was going to be writing about Gatsby, a man who falsified his life history; with this in mind, he could insert elements of false history into his narrator's, Nick Carraway's, family myth and allow Nick to be aware of them. He could have just given Nick an ordinary family history, but by paralleling elements from Gatsby's story he's emphasizing the novel's themes. When you articulate the intentions for your story or essay or memoir, and are aware of the themes in your piece, you can create parallels in background summaries (and elsewhere) that will help develop your themes. If you decide that the theme of your short story is, for example, the brevity of life, you might give your character a background history in which her parents died young. Know your intention and then build it into your story via summaries as well as scenes.

Another example of background summary doing double duty is contained in Richard Selzer's *Letters to a Young Doctor*. This passage begins the essay and precedes the tale of Selzer's superior, Dr. Franciscus, performing free corrective surgery in Honduras in which a young, deformed, Mestiza girl dies midoperation:

> Dr. Franciscus was the archetype of the professor of surgery—tall, vigorous, muscular, as precise in his technique as he was impeccable in his dress. Each day a clean lab coat monkishly starched, that sort of thing. I doubt if he ever read books. One book only, that of the human body, took the place of all the others. He never

raised his eyes from it. He read it like a printed page as though he knew that in the calligraphy there just beneath the skin were all the secrets of the world.

Rather than carry themes, this background summary, along with giving general information about Dr. Franciscus, *sets up an expectation* about Franciscus's obsessive, perfectionist character that will be shattered by the girl's death, an expectation that is necessary for the turn of events to have full impact. If you wish to set up expectations about a person's character in order to shatter them, you first must know that your piece will turn on a contrast between the impression a person gives and an event that reveals another aspect of the character that contradicts that initial impression. The event, of course, should occur in a scene, but your background summary can establish the initial impression that you will later crush in the scene. For example, if you are writing about a homeless man encountering a person from his earlier life, the meeting would occur in a scene, but your background summary could give us insight into the life he led before he was homeless or into his former relationship with the person he is going to meet again.

Background summary placed at the beginning of a work can let us in on the history of a character and also set the story in motion, as in this excerpt from the first page of Abby Frucht's novel *Life Before Death*:

> I am such an insufferable optimist, and for the longest time, not including that awful day five years ago when my parents were killed and I turned thirty-five, life seemed to be moving in such a routine, predictable, responsible way that when I discovered the lump in my breast my first thought was that all sorts of new, unexpected, interesting things would finally start happening to me.

In this brief excerpt, a single sentence, we learn that the narrator's parents were killed in a car accident; she is now forty, and, except for the accident, her life has always been predictable; she's so optimistic that finding a lump in her breast seems to her an interesting rather than a terrifying event. The simple use of the word *finally* lets us know that her current life must be quite dull. And, despite the casual voice, we have just learned of the novel's catalytic event—the discovery of what will turn out to be a cancerous tumor. This huge discovery is relayed, not in a developed scene, but through background information. Surely this is an unusual approach to starting a novel, but Frucht carries it off through the distinctive and appealing voice of her narrator. I include it here not because I'm encouraging everyone to try this difficult approach but for you to see the wide-ranging possibilities of background summary, and how it can serve you in multiple ways beyond simply delivering the history of people and places.

Background information doesn't have to come at the beginning of a novel or story or essay, as it does in the Frucht and Selzer excerpts. It can be inserted elsewhere when needed. Pico Iyer, in his book *Falling Off the Map: Some Lonely Places of the World,* gives us a glimpse into the background of his Vietnamese travel guide to support his point that the general populace in postwar, Communist Vietnam is not particularly interested in politics:

> For most of the people in Hanoi, with their cash-register quickness and low-key patriotism, there are more urgent concerns than ideology. My guide to the city, a friendly, cherubic fellow in a baseball cap, with a ready grin, had been a Vietcong platoon commander for four years, but even his accounts of the war were matter-of-fact and hardly partisan ... The present moment, with its promise of economic openness and its freedom from strife, was

the sunniest period in his forty years, he said. But still he
started every sentence with "The problem is that ... "

Here, midway through a piece on visiting Vietnam, Iyer convinces us that his guide, a former North Vietnamese warrior, isn't tied to Communist ideology. He even tells us that the guide thought his most difficult moment wasn't in the war but when he visited Bulgaria and was told by an eighteen-year-old girl that she loved him. Iyer makes the man, a minor character, an individual, with physical characteristics, emotions, and memories. The guide's background adds texture and depth to this piece. Iyer uses the man to support his point about the lack of Communist zeal in Vietnam, but he doesn't just *use* him; he gives him a personality and a voice. He makes him human.

We often tend to take shortcuts with minor characters in our writing, not bothering to give them histories or feelings that if provided, might enrich the overall work. Of course I'm not suggesting that every character have a genealogy attached! But remember that not only your protagonist or your other main characters deserve backgrounds that will make them more real on the page. The key in using background summary for minor characters is very careful selection—you want a few words to work hard for you in creating as rounded a character as possible. Iyer gives us the picture of a "cherubic fellow in a baseball cap" and tells us that the guide was a Vietcong platoon commander. This contrast between appearance and the guide's history gives texture; the man is no longer two-dimensional. In background summary you can summarize dialogue, as Iyer does, when he tells us that the guide has said that the present moment is the "sunniest in his forty years." In a few lines you can deepen a minor character and allow him to live on the page.

Background summary can also do double duty by providing details of setting and characterization without a specific scene. Lois-Ann Yamanaka's young narrator, in her novel *Blu's Hanging*, tells us:

> It's so hot in this town that babies wear diapers only, men go without shirts, windows and doors stay wide open, and people seek out the shade of a mango tree, or a lanai where there's breeze. Inside, ceiling fans whir and standing fans with blue-cool plastic blades collect oily dust in a blue-gray blur.
>
> That's why Mama said steam, don't fry—it's so hot here that when you're standing over a pan of bubbling oil, your sweat rolls off your eyebrow, lands in the hot oil, and wham, it shoots you right in the face. *Teach me how to be a Mama too.* I'm learning the hard way. Never reach for the salt over a pan of frying chicken. Hot oil spat at my underarm for doing that.

From this summary, we get a picture of the place in which the adolescent narrator lives, an impoverished Hawaiian neighborhood where no one has air-conditioning. But the novelist slides smoothly, within the summary, into a picture of the young protagonist struggling with the responsibility of feeding her younger siblings after her mother's death, a literally and figuratively painful experience. The background summary has filled us in on both the physical and the emotional landscape of the narrator.

You can use background summary as a means of describing a place, and, if you so desire, the emotional situation of your character(s), by including details that exist *not in a specific scene, a specific time*, but as part of the overall imaginative landscape of your piece. For example, I could tell you that I grew up in a big old colonial house in New Hampshire but that wouldn't be giving you much more than the location of my childhood. But if I tell you that my childhood house had a dark screened porch on one side, facing a row of rhododendrons whose bees frightened me and that beyond it was a dark pine forest in which a strange man once appeared, you'll get a certain dark and scary impression. If I tell you that the other side of the house had a bright enclosed sunporch facing a row of lilac bushes that I liked to sit under so I could sip the nectar from the little cross-shaped blossoms, you'd have an entirely different impression of my childhood. If I tell you that both were true you might begin to get a sense of the contradictions within that house. Here I'm using background summary to provide a literal and symbolic setting, establishing a physical and emotional landscape.

To do this in your own writing, consider the particular details that best describe the place in which your piece is set. Which details will give a clear picture of what matters or mattered to your characters—which details reflect their emotional states? What aspects of background setting might contain symbolic as well as factual weight? Of course, to do this, you have to return to that old standby: intention. You need to know what the effect is that you're striving for before you can choose the best components to realize your intention.

COMPRESSING TIME

Another traditional use of summary is to condense events. If someone at a party asked you what you'd been up to since he'd last seen you, you wouldn't bore him with every time you went to the store, took a shower, saw a movie, took a nap, talked to your mother. You'd choose highlights. You might even offer information that showed you in a way you wanted your audience to see you. If you were talking to an old girlfriend or boyfriend who dumped you, you might choose events that stressed your accomplishments —"Oh, let's see, I got my law degree from Stanford and a few years later I made partner. My wife, Karen, is an editor at *Vogue* now. We just recently had our second child … " If you were talking to a good friend, you might tell him about your bout with depression and how it took you a few years and a number of bad choices before you found a therapist who really helped. You'd pick out the most relevant events suited to the occasion and the audience. You'd compress time to highlight only the events you wanted to relay. This is the same thing that we do as writers when we condense time in our stories through the use of summary. We not only compress background information via summary, as above, but we can compress events that occur between scenes.

Given that you don't want to write a scene to cover every event that happens in the lives of your characters or to the people and places around them, summary allows you to *tell rather than show* when you want to cover a span of time in a relatively brief amount of space on the page. Note: You compress time through summary when *the span of events* is more important to the tale than are the *individual events*. This does not mean that you relay the events without enough specific details to make them come alive (you wouldn't want to write as generically as I did in the conversational examples above), but you wouldn't devote the same amount of space to each event mentioned in the summary as you would if they warranted scenes. The essence of the summarized time period is what you're after. With the old lover the gist is "see how well I've done without you over the past ten years?" With the old friend the gist is "I had some problems but I've gotten some help and I'm doing okay now."

You can see an example of this in an excerpt from James McBride's memoir *The Color of Water: A Black Man's Tribute to His White Mother* in which McBride summarizes the manner in which his mother and stepfather met and began a relationship:

> My stepfather worked as a furnace fireman for the New York City Housing Authority, fixing and maintaining the huge boilers that heated the Red Hook Housing Projects where we lived then. He and Mommy met a few months

after my biological father died; Ma was selling church dinners in the plaza in front of our building at 811 Hicks Street when my stepfather came by and bought a rib dinner. The next week he came back and bought another, then another and another. He must have been getting sick eating all those ribs. Finally one afternoon he came by where she was selling the church dinners and asked Ma, "Do you go to the movies?"

"Yeah," she said. "But I got eight kids and they go to the movies too."

"You got enough for a baseball team," he said.

He married her and made the baseball team his own, adding four more kids to make it an even twelve.

In this passage McBride begins with a general statement about his stepfather's employment. He locates us in time but not a scene with "a few months after." Then he neatly compresses a week ("the next week he came back") and either days or weeks—we can't quite tell how many days separated each of the four rib dinners mentioned but it doesn't matter. He slips into a specifically located brief scene with "Finally one afternoon ... " and a few lines of dialogue, before slipping back into summary and compressing years with the line "He married her ... adding four more kids to make it an even twelve." In thirteen lines many years pass and we get not only the story of the meeting of a man and a woman but the fact that they married, he accepted her eight children, and they had four more kids together. Imagine the space it would take to write all of that in scenes! Because the focus of this memoir is McBride's white mother, her secret history as the daughter of a rabbi, and his own struggle for identity in a mixed-race family, the story of his stepfather's meeting and courting his mother needs to be compressed.

You should make special note of the locating tags McBride uses to keep the reader clear that time is passing—"a few months after" ... "the next week" and so on. "Adding four more kids" succinctly lets us know that years have gone by (unless they had quadruplets, which they didn't). When you compress time through summary make sure your reader comes along with you by using tags or choosing details that express time passing.

Ernest Hemingway, in his story "The End of Something," actually uses details to evoke the passage of time in a compressed manner. Note how the run of events is more important than any of the individual events as he describes, in summary, the dismantling of a logging town (ellipses mine):

> In the old days Horton's Bay was a lumbering town. No one who lived in it was out of sound of the big saws in the mill by the lake. Then one year there were no more logs ... The lumber schooners came into the bay and were loaded with the cut of the mill that stood stacked in the yard ... The big mill building had all its machinery ... taken out and hoisted on board one of the schooners ... Ten years later there was nothing of the mill left except the broken white limestone of its foundations showing through the swampy second growth ...

This summary covers decades in a few paragraphs. Hemingway accomplishes this through the shift in details. First there are the noisy saws. Then there are no more logs. Then boats took away all the stacked lumber and the mill machinery. Finally there is nothing but the broken foundation peeking through the brush. Of course, Hemingway also uses locator tags such as "then one year" and "ten years later" as well as the details of the dismantling to compress the passage of time.

Interestingly, the summarized description of the decline and disappearance of the lumber town in this story parallels, through telling about the end of an era, the end of the romantic relationship between the teenaged Nick Adams and his girlfriend,

Marjorie, who have come to spend the day fishing in Horton's Bay. Like the earlier excerpt from Fitzgerald's *The Great Gatsby*, this paragraph of summary sets up themes to follow.

The McBride and Hemingway examples have both compressed time while giving background in the form of summary. You can also compress time as your narrative moves forward through the use of summary. For example, if you're writing a scene in which a child is lost in a department store and your next heightened moment (i.e., scene) is the lost child's parents arguing over whose fault it was that the child was lost, you might want to compress the time that occurs between the scene at the store and the argument, including the drive home from the store, picking up older children after school, getting dinner ready, etc. If you decide that none of these intervening events warrants a scene, you might just sum them up by saying something along the lines of:

> Elizabeth continued to berate herself for taking her eyes off Jilly for the rest of the day. When she sat in the parents' pickup line outside Hillview Elementary waiting for Jimmy and Ellen, she couldn't help thinking none of the other mothers would have done something as stupid or irresponsible; she could barely listen to the kids' chatter or their arguments over which TV show they would watch, she was so busy loathing herself. And she couldn't stop running into Jilly's room to check on her while she napped even though she burned the burgers and scorched the rice.

The narrative continues, while being summarized, leading up to the next scene.

You can compress time in your work in a straightforward manner ("A year later my family moved to Massachusetts") or in a more lively manner using details to convey time passing ("In high school Kaylee could have gotten a spot on the varsity mall shopping team; in college she grew more serious and started talking about American Imperialism and Fair Trade; she considered joining the Peace Corps). Either way you must keep your reader located as time leaps forward.

There are dangers associated with using summary to compress time. The first is that you might pack so much past event into the summary that your reader gets lost. This can be ameliorated by using the time locator tags or time-related details as shown above. The second pitfall is that your summary contains so much information that none of it makes an impact on the reader. To avoid the second problem you need to be clear on your overall intention and choose *only* events and details that support that intention. This is as true for nonfiction as for fiction. You must have a good reason for including the components that you've chosen in your summary. Don't just put them in because "they happened" or, in fiction, could have happened. Compression means selection, and selection allows the included components to have maximum impact. If you read the Hemingway story "The End of Something" you'll see that Hemingway compresses the history of Horton's Bay as a parallel to the end of the relationship between the two young people. He doesn't compress time in order to give the story of the evolution of the fish in Horton's Bay, which would have no bearing on the story at hand. He doesn't compress time to tell you about other girls that Nick Adams might have taken fishing in the past. He focuses his summary on details that will emphasize or reverberate with the themes of "The End of Something." Hemingway's intention informed what he included in his summary and yours should too.

GENERAL TIME

We've been talking about compressing time through summary and for the most part, although we haven't been dealing with scenes, we've still been dealing with specific time periods.

However, summaries can be used when you wish to write about events, information, and ideas that do not take place in specific times. I call this "general time"—a kind of nonspecific "stepping out of time." Nonscene memories, repeated actions, reflections, etc., can be inserted within ongoing scenes, when appropriate, or they can stand on their own as essential summary that enriches the ongoing narrative. This may sound a little mystical, but it is pretty down to earth.

When might you use general time in your own summaries? Anytime you wish to convey information or ideas or events that aren't tied to a specific time. If your narrator thinks something as prosaic as, *The cat will probably have kittens; I wish I'd gotten her spayed,* that thought can take place in a summary that uses general time. (It *could* be put into a scene but it doesn't have to be. "Gerald wanted to marry Esmerelda." That's general time—we don't know when he's having this thought. We just know it as a part of the character of Gerald, a piece of the story that exists outside of a scene.)

Here's an example of an informative passage in an essay by Annie Dillard called "Living Like Weasels" that uses general time:

> A weasel is wild. Who knows what he thinks? He sleeps in his underground den, his tail draped over his nose. Sometimes he lives in his den for two days without leaving. Outside, he stalks rabbits, mice, muskrats, and birds, killing more bodies than he can eat warm, and often dragging the carcasses home.

Dillard isn't describing a particular weasel here at a specific time; she is telling us about weasels in general. She uses the above excerpt to start her essay, which soon moves into a scene (set in a specific time/specific place) about an individual weasel she observed. Dillard then returns to summary using general time as she makes a connection between the weasel she witnessed and her desire to live "in the physical senses" and "without bias or motive."

Lest you think this kind of summary in the form of "musing" set in general time is only the province of creative nonfiction, it occurs in fiction as well. In Jess Row's short story "The Secrets of Bats," the narrator's thoughts exist in the ether of general time:

> I've come to see my life as a radiating circle of improbabilities that grow from each other, like ripples in water around a dropped stone. That I became a high school English teacher, that I live in Hong Kong. That a city can be a mirage, hovering above the ground: skyscrapers built on mountainsides, islands swallowed in fog for days.

Summaries that use general time can be prosaic or lyrical, they can be high flown or straight forward factual, as simple as "I like popcorn" or "Jimmy attends Dartmouth College." All they need is to exist outside of a specific span of time.

REPEATED TIME

Summary is uniquely suited to describing actions and events that happen repeatedly. In repeated time summary, the emphasis is on the recurrent nature of the action rather than an event deserving an individual scene. You are telling, not showing, these repeated actions. It would be tedious to show these actions over and over again through scenes or even to summarize them each time they happened. You wouldn't want to read a version of every time a character took the train to work. It's enough to know that "Fred commuted by train to the city most days, except when his wife had an appointment with her dermatologist; then they drove in." The use of summary to show repeated events is efficient; it can help to maintain reader interest by paring away extraneous material. Repeated time comes under the umbrella of general time.

There are a number of techniques for indicating repeated actions via summary, including the use of conditional verbs, pluralizing certain words, and using words that indicate repetition, as shown below.

Conditional verbs are frequently used to establish repeated actions, as in this excerpt from Evan S. Connell's novel *Mrs. Bridge* (italics mine):

> Mrs. Bridge *could* never learn what Ruth did in the evenings, or where she went; she entered the house quietly, sometimes not long before dawn.

Lawrence Sutin, in his book *A Postcard Memoir,* also uses the conditional to summarize repeated actions (italics mine):

> I *wouldn't* come out to meet company in the living room if they offered fruit or sugar cookies. I *would* if they offered chocolate. I *would* if it was my birthday or Hanukkah and they had presents. I *would* if my parents came looking for me and insisted. Craven as I was, my parents *would* kindly give in after I'd made my brief hellos and how are yous and let me hide in the basement where I learned to make sparks pounding nails into the concrete floor hard.

In addition to the conditional, particular time-related adverbs or phrases can establish repeated actions, such as *always, frequently, often, sometimes, used to, once in a while,* etc. This is another excerpt from Evan S. Connell's *Mrs. Bridge* (italics mine):

> If she bought a book it was almost *always* one of three things: a best-seller she had heard about or seen advertised,

a self-improvement book, or a book by a Kansas City author no matter what it was about.

Pluralizing particular words can turn a description or action into repeated time. Note Robert Olmstead's use of "certain nights" and "Such nights" below in this excerpt from "Cody's Story":

> It was a good life for the two gypsy loggers, even in the winter, when on certain nights the dark silence heaved open with the sound of hardwoods cracking and snapping from the cold within their very heartwood. Such nights Cody would sit bolt straight in bed and curse silently to himself. G.R. was merely thankful it didn't get as cold as it used to in the old days.

Tobias Wolff, in his memoir *This Boy's Life*, makes it clear that his abusive stepfather Dwight's actions are repeated through his language choices, which include the phrase "a study," implying an ongoing process, and time tags, such as "during the day," "in the evening," "late at night," and through a litany of complaints:

> Dwight made a study of me. He thought about me during the day while he grunted over the engines of trucks and generators, and in the evening while he watched me eat, and late at night while he sat heavy-lidded at the kitchen table with a pint of Old Crow and package of Camels to support him in his deliberations. He shared his findings as they came to him. The trouble with me was, I thought I was going to get through life without doing any work. The trouble with me was, I thought I was smarter than everyone else. The trouble with me was, I thought other people couldn't tell what I was thinking. The trouble with me was, I didn't think.

The repetitious summarized dialogue makes Dwight's complaints seem like a broken record. In an individual scene we'd have to hear a character say (or think), "You always say that!" Wolff uses summary to give us, efficiently and subtly, the repeated action and his adult judgment of Dwight even though he's an adolescent at the time of the repeated actions. As a side note, the level of detail in this commentary on his stepfather gives this summary the vividness of scene: Dwight's grunting over engines, heavy-lidded at the table with a pint of Old Crow and a package of Camels to support him in his deliberations. (Here Wolff uses adult diction to heighten the irony.) Through Dwight's "findings"—again, the adult wording heightens the irony that this dull-witted, mean man could ever find anything—and through the summarized dialogue, "The trouble with me" litany, we also get the contradictions in Dwight's repeated observations that reveal his character.

As you can see from the above examples, you have a number of techniques at your disposal when you wish to describe repeated actions without having to create scenes for each occurrence. The use of conditional verbs (would, could) and adverbs of time (always, every, sometimes) are the simplest and most commonly used approaches. If you're feeling more ambitious you can try indicating repetition through carefully selected phrases that indicate repetition or summarized, repetitious dialogue, as Wolff does. A useful exercise to that end is to notice ways in which other writers indicate repeated actions without using the conditional or repetition-indicating adverbs, and then try a few. Here's one:

My mother alternated peanut butter and grape jelly with cream cheese and grape jelly on Wonder bread in my school lunches with comforting regularity. On the first day of sixth grade I opened my Archie and Veronica lunch box to find a stack of round white crackers and a triangular lump of runny cheese that smelled like the ammonia she used to wash the windows. Something was happening and it wasn't good. The brie, as she called it, was followed by oily pink smoked salmon, macadamia nuts, little black squares of rye bread, and a disgusting green fruit with gluey black seeds. "Be adventurous," she admonished me. I couldn't find anyone in the lunch room who would trade.

This example breaks briefly into scene (the first day of sixth grade) but then returns to repeated time with the array of adult foods that show up in the lunch box and the failed attempts at trading lunches that surely happened more than once. It also includes another technique you can use to indicate repeated time—listing. Here, in the context of the excerpt, the list of odd school lunches describes repeated disappointment.

DEVELOPING CHARACTER IN SUMMARIES

Just as in scenes, summaries provide the opportunity to explore character through observing a person's demeanor and actions or entering that person's interior world, only without being tied to a particular incident. Characters even can be made individual obliquely, via objects and details described in summary. (Think of what the car you drive, the foods you prefer, the way you dress at home reveal about you.)

BEHAVIOR AND DESCRIPTION

You've already learned how to develop character in scenes by *showing* how a person acts and looks, smells, sounds, etc. You can do the same in summaries but in this case you're *telling* your reader about your character in general or repeated time rather than in a specific time. Revealing character through behavior and description in summary allows you or your narrator to tell the reader important information about characters before we see them in scenes. This is time-saving and often useful in informing the reader's understanding of a scene that will arise after the summary. However, summarized description and behavior should never be *generic* just because it occurs in general time. That means you'll need to select individual characteristics that not only fit your character's personality but tell who that character is. If I summarize that the mother of the child in the school lunch excerpt above was unhappy at home, regretted not having gone to college, and longed to raise herself from her middle-class boredom, the summary is bland and not particularly revealing. If I tell you that the mother had recently joined a Great Books Reading Club and talked relentlessly about meeting people of "superior intellect" and "sophistication" compared to the couples from his father's insurance office who used to come by for barbecue, and that she'd begun replacing mac and cheese with oddities such as sole meuniere at dinner, that she handed his father a glass of white wine instead of a beer, and broke into tears or stomped out when no one appreciated her efforts, I'd still be summarizing but you'd get a much clearer picture of what was going on with the mother and the family. Specific, individualized actions and details enrich summary just as they enrich scenes, and they reveal character in both.

In Joyce Carol Oates's terrifying story "Where Are You Going, Where Have You Been?" the teenage protagonist Connie reveals herself, through summarized, repeated actions:

> She wore a pullover jersey blouse that looked one way when she was at home and another way when she was away from home. Everything about her had two sides to it, one for home and one for anywhere that was not home: her walk that could be childlike and bobbing, or languid

enough to make anyone think she was hearing music in her head, her mouth which was pale and smirking most of the time, but bright and pink on these evenings out, her laugh which was cynical and drawling at home ... but high-pitched and nervous anywhere else ...

In addition to using specific details about Connie's appearance, Oates uses a list of verbs to define Connie's two-sided character both in and outside of this excerpt: scuffing, leaning, whispering, laughing, smirking, drawling, bobbing, jingling. She layers adjectives and nouns: pale, bright pink, bracelets, ballerina slippers, blond, jersey, cynical, nervous. Together the verbs, nouns, and adjectives give us a clear picture of this character *in motion, in action.* The actions are repeated in no specific time frame—this is how Connie generally looks and behaves.

When you are developing character through summary, consider the individual but *habitual* aspects of that character's behavior and appearance. Does he dress in low-slung cargo pants or Dockers? Does he smoke cigarettes awkwardly, like a kid learning, or is he robustly athletic, often seen spinning about the roadways in spandex shorts on his racing bike? Does he squash spiders or carry ladybugs outside when he finds them? Consider the verbs and adjectives you might use in describing this guy. Reach past the obvious ones for the ones that carry the most weight. This awareness of who your characters are in general time, not just in scenes, will help you as well as your readers come to know them fully.

INTERIOR LIFE

Characters have interior lives, just as you and everyone you know have them. In Section I, I discussed the ways in which interior life can be revealed in scenes. But there's no reason you can't explore your characters' interior lives in general and repeated time, in summaries. Moreover, doing so can add a great deal of depth to your characters, sometimes more depth than a scene alone could convey. For example, in her novel *Anagrams,* Lorrie Moore *tells* us about her protagonist Benna's loneliness:

> Benna misses everyone.
>
> Benna misses everyone she's ever known and spends her weekends writing long letters, extravagant in their warmth, signed always, "Lots of love, Benna." She used to pay attention to how letters people wrote her were signed, but now she tries not to notice when the letters she receives close with "Take Care" or "Be Well" or "See you Christmas"—or sometimes simply "Moi." Look for "Love," she jokes to herself, and you will never find it.

This isn't a scene; Benna isn't just writing one letter at one specific time. The actions are repeated and it is in this repetition that we learn that Benna continually tries to avoid the truth—no one seems to love and need her—and that she copes through desperate attempts at affection and sad humor. If we had a scene in which Benna wrote one letter or one in which she received a letter and studied the way the letter writer ended it with "Take Care," we wouldn't understand half of what we receive from this summary in which we learn about Benna's *habitual* letter writing behavior and her *continued* attempt not to notice the impersonal sign-offs from "everyone she's ever known."

Moore explores Benna's interior life—her emotional make-up—by flat out *telling* us that Benna misses everyone and then by further developing this statement with the example of Benna's repeated outward behavior (letter writing) and repeated emotional state—ignoring the evidence of indifferent responses to her letters. Moore also uses humor by letting us in on Benna's joke about "Looking for Love" at the bottom of a letter—an event that is also not attached to a scene. It's a joke but it's a pointed one. Here's a case in which telling beats out showing for developing character.

You can tell your reader about your characters' internal lives in summary by directly addressing their emotional states or desires such as: Benna misses everyone. George often feels unaccountably angry. Susan fantasizes about being a pilot every time she drives past the airport. Whenever he talked to his mother on the phone, Ralph felt like rolling over the edge of his balcony.

You'll need to follow up that direct statement with more detailed information or the straightforward observation will come across as rather bald. The line "Benna misses everyone" alone wouldn't have nearly the impact that the full summary about her letter writing and receiving does. It wouldn't let the reader in on how Benna copes with her loneliness. Think about ways to continue the summary so your reader learns significant information about your character's (or narrator's) emotions. Ask yourself "Why?" Why does Ralph want to roll off his balcony after talking to his mother? What does he actually feel about her? Guilt? Frustration? Burdened? Angry? Helpless love (perhaps she has dementia)? All of the above? Now think of the "How." How might your character/narrator acknowledge/act out/suppress these emotions as Benna acts out her loneliness through the extravagantly warm letters to acquaintances?

At this point you might be wondering why you don't just *show* Ralph getting off the phone and considering rolling off his balcony in a scene. Why summarize? The answer is that Ralph *always* feels this way after talking to his mother. Once is not enough. Summary allows you to explore the emotion over a span of time. Even if it isn't a habitual emotion, it's an emotion that happens in general, not specific time.

The internal lives of characters can be revealed through their musings (a form of summary). In Evan S. Connell's novel built of vignettes, *Mr. Bridge,* Mr. Bridge's character is revealed by his musings that take the form of a summing up of the past year:

> Now another year was ending. The year had been good and he regretted the end of it, but he felt pleased that it was concluding without sickness in the family and with indications that the worst of the Depression might be over. The children were growing up nearly as he hoped they would and his wife was content.

In the stuffy Mr. Bridge's rather bland, summarized musings we are offered a detailed picture of his formal, impersonal feelings about his family—"the children were growing up *nearly* as he'd hoped." His lack of compassion is revealed further as he goes on to revile Roosevelt and the poor that "stand around on street corners complaining and waiting for the government to feed them." Through summary, Mr. Bridge reveals his *attitude* toward family and the world. This attitude can be seen in his use of the words "nearly" and "complaining and waiting for the government to feed them." Notice that these bland musings are the character's, not the narrator's.

In your own work you can capture the attitude of a character or narrator by careful choice of words. If your narrator thinks about a person who is always "lurking" around, the word lurking will convey an attitude that differs substantially than if the narrator mused that someone was always "hanging" around or "waiting" around or "appearing unexpectedly." You have only words to work with; make them count when it comes to revealing interior life.

Sometimes the summarized musings of a character or narrator expose more than just an attitude—they display psychological irregularities and abnormalities. In Mark Haddon's novel *The Curious Incident of the Dog in the Night-Time*, the narrator Christopher is autistic. His unspoken thoughts reveal his struggles with deciphering ordinary human behaviors. Moreover, the arrangement of his thoughts betray his inability to make ordinary mental associations. His own associations are peculiar to his condition as well as his talents and his syntax has a certain repetitive and robotic quality that goes with his neurological deficits:

> A lie is when you say something happened which didn't happen. But there is only ever one thing which happened at a particular time and a particular place. And there are an infinite number of things which didn't happen at that time and that place. And if I think about something which didn't happen I start thinking about all the other things which didn't happen … and even writing this makes me feel shaky and scared, like I do when I'm standing on the top of a very tall building and there are thousands of houses and cars and people below me and my head is so full of all these things that I'm afraid that I'm going to forget to stand up straight and hang on to the rail and I'm going to fall over and be killed.
>
> This is another reason why I don't like proper novels, because they are lies about things which didn't happen and they make me feel shaky and scared.

Mark Haddon could have used a flatter form of summary here. He could have told us that Christopher's autism makes him unable to understand the nuances of truth and lies and therefore incapable of enjoying fiction. But in this case, Haddon allows us to explore Christopher's mental machinations through his own musings—giving us a window into his interior life and the unusual ways his mind works. Because the author is using summary here, Christopher is speaking about himself in general and repeated time rather than referring to an individual event via scene. Christopher *always* tells the truth because he can't understand lies.

While the characters are telling us about themselves in general or repeated time through musing, they are, in effect, *showing* us how their minds work. Paradoxically, this form of summary contains both showing and telling, though there is no scene involved. This is particularly important if you're writing about someone with psychological differences or deviances— autistic like Christopher; mentally handicapped like Benjy in Faulkner's novel *The Sound and the Fury*; deranged as in Patrick McCabe's novel *The Butcher Boy*; drunk or substance abusing in numerous memoirs and works of fiction; obsessive, or even crazed by romantic yearning, as in *Endless Love*. The musings of these characters or narrators will show your reader a great deal about *how* they think, not just *what* they think.

How can you capture the irregularities in a narrator's or character's thought processes through summarized musing? First you have to identify what makes that person's thinking different from "normal" people. Does the person think repeatedly about who has touched doorknobs and whether or not those doorknob touchers washed their hands after going to the bathroom? Or does she garble her thoughts and veer from sentimentality to anger as a drunk might? Is it an adult with a child's mistaken trust of strangers? (Or is it, in fact, a child, with the attention to sensory detail that children possess?) After clarifying the difference in your own mind, you must perform a feat of imagination and inhabit that person. If you are writing memoir, not fiction, but you are writing about your life from your perspective as a child, you must essentially do the same thing. You are writing from the mind of someone quite different from your adult self. But how do you inhabit that other?

I often find it useful, with fiction, when I'm having difficulty getting inside a character ("normal" or not) to free write from the first-person point of view of that person, even if the novel or story is in third person. While I may, and usually do, throw out all of the free writing, it helps me to capture something essential about the way that person views the world that carries over into the writing I intend to save. If you are a memoirist, you can use much the same exercise by free writing from your child-self or otherwise earlier point of view. It's a way of tapping into your subconscious understanding of who that person is/was. It helps to take the pressure off by thinking of the writing as an exercise you'll probably throw out. You'll be surprised at what results if you don't judge and just let the words come. Don't worry about whether or not you are writing summarized musing or if you slip into a scene—just keep it coming. The object is to find your way into the character/narrator's interior life.

EXTERIOR AND INTERIOR

Rarely does a piece of creative prose rely *only* on interior or *only* on exterior indications of character. In chapter 4, I discussed the combination of behavior, dialogue, and interior monologue in scene, using Victoria Redel's novel *Loverboy* as an example (see page 61). You can combine the elements of behavior, description, dialogue, and internal monologue to reveal character fully in summary, when you don't want to be tied to a specific scene.

Tim O'Brien's brilliant novel *The Things They Carried* is unusual in the extent to which it employs summary to explore characters' inner and outer lives. In fact, the story depends on summary and has very few scenes; its intention is to load you down with the weight of what a platoon of soldiers had to carry, both physically and emotionally. It is about a particular platoon, but it strives for a universality of soldierly experience—or, rather, the experiences of American soldiers in Vietnam—that exceeds the experiences of these individual men, and the use of summary helps to convey that universality:

> The things they carried were largely determined by neces-
> sity. Among the necessities or near necessities were P38
> can openers, pocket knives, heat tabs, wrist watches, dog
> tags, mosquito repellent, chewing gum, candy, cigarettes,

salt tablets, packets of Kool-Aid, lighters, matches, sewing kits, Military Payment Certificates, C rations, and two or three canteens of water. Together these items weighed between fifteen and twenty pounds, depending upon a man's habits or rate of metabolism. Henry Dobbins, who was a big man, carried extra rations; he was especially fond of canned peaches in heavy syrup over pound cake. Dave Jensen, who practiced field hygiene, carried a toothbrush, dental floss, and several hotel-size bars of soap he'd stolen on R&R in Sydney, Australia. Ted Lavender, who was scared, carried tranquilizers until he was shot in the head outside the village of Than Khe in mid-April.

... Until he was shot, Ted Lavender carried six or seven ounces of premium dope, which for him was a necessity. Mitchell Sanders, the RTO, carried condoms. Norman Bowker carried a diary. Rat Kiley carried comic books. Kiowa, a devout Baptist, carried an illustrated New Testament that had been presented to him by his father, who taught Sunday school in Oklahoma City, Oklahoma. As a hedge against bad times, however, Kiowa also carried his grandmother's distrust of the white man, his grandfather's old hunting hatchet.

What's so unusual and striking in this story is that although the platoon members are characterized via objects, they are individualized and humanized. There is nothing vague about O'Brien's summary sections that explore the exterior and interior lives of his characters. They are detailed, even more detailed than the scenes in this story.

O'Brien reveals character through exterior detail—the specific things the men carry tell something about their concerns—and he reveals the emotional lives of these characters by telling us why some of the men carried what they did—Ted Lavender carried tranquillizers because he was fearful; Kiowa was devout but also distrustful of whites. Both the interior and exterior details exist in general time, the world of the summary, which exists outside of a specific scene and signifies continuing activities. O'Brien employs the technique of listing to convey just how much these men carry.

You will probably want to combine elements of the exterior and interior lives of your characters or your narrator as a means of making them real and recognizable to your reader. To identify their interior thoughts, you can use the first-person free-writing method suggested above, if you wish, and elements of their exterior life—appearance, demeanor, behavior. What does this person wear? How does he move or speak? Where does she shop and what for? What does he do if he encounters a child or a dog? What does she watch on television, or does she even watch television at all? And so on—ask questions of your characters to find out who they are. Then use those answers to tell your readers who this person is and how she thinks generally.

Of course, you'll be narrowing the time span to some degree—O'Brien was writing about the members of a platoon on active duty in Vietnam, not these guys at other times in their lives. And you might be telling about your character or narrator at a particular *era* in her life—as a child, in high school, young adulthood, old age, etc. But you'll still be telling your reader how that person acts and thinks (within that broad time framework) *in general*. The irony is that to tell how someone behaves and feels *in general* you have to get specific if you want your summary to have impact, just as O'Brien gets specific in the details that characterize the men in the platoon. You won't be specific in time and place in the same way as in a scene, but specific in detail and emotion. Your narrator, for example, doesn't just like apples more than oranges; your narrator despises all citrus fruit since the day he opened a jar of pickled kumquats that he'd been forbidden to try and discovered that the forbidden can be bitter and sour, not sweet.

REFLECTION

$\mathcal{S}$ummary has another important use besides compressing time, providing background, and filling us in on characters. It is through *reflective* summary, or *reflection*, that we get to hear a distinct narrative voice that ponders and comments on the action or characters. A reflective narrator can even bring in outside material to enlarge our understanding of topics even tangentially related to the story. We've been so ingrained with the message "show, don't tell" that we forget that some of the most powerful writers have strong reflective voices that ponder and interpret people and events.

When Charles Dickens, in *A Tale of Two Cities,* says, "It was the best of times; it was the worst of times … it was the season of Light, it was the season of Darkness … " he has telegrammed for the reader the paradoxes of the French Revolution. Of course he's speaking in large abstractions and you wouldn't want to read (or write) a book made up only of abstractions, and Dickens certainly gets into the specifics of his story soon after this reflective introduction. But this is an example of summary in the form of authorial commentary that enriches rather than draws energy away from the text. Dickens reflects in a manner that gets you intrigued so you are hungry to find out how the story will live out the ideas raised by his introduction.

But it isn't just the writers of classic nineteenth-century lit-erature such as Dickens and Tolstoy who engage in reflection. Many modern and contemporary writers do as well. John Up-dike, John Cheever, Maya Angelou, David Foster Wallace, Toni Morrison, Michael Chabon, Sherman Alexie, Amy Tan, Barbara Kingsolver, and countless other fiction writers, memoirists, and personal essayists use reflection to greater or lesser degrees.

Webster's dictionary defines reflection as: *a thought, idea, or opinion formed or a remark made as a result of meditation; a consideration of some subject matter, idea, or purpose.* And the verb to reflect is defined as *to think quietly and calmly.* Consid-eration, meditation, calm and quiet thinking—a reflective narra-tive voice acts as guide and interpreter through a tale; it's a voice that says it's not enough to know what happened, I'll attempt to tell you why it happened or what it means.

So who cares, you might ask. Who wants to know what I think about the story? Thoreau, in his first page of *Walden,* in the chapter entitled "Economy," provides an argument for the value of his own perceptions and reflections:

> I should not talk so much about myself if there were any-body else whom I knew as well. Unfortunately, I am con-fined to this theme by the narrowness of my experience. Moreover, I, on my side, require of every writer, first or last, a simple and sincere account of his own life, and not merely what he has heard of other men's lives; some such account as he would send to his kindred from a distant land; for if he has lived sincerely, it must have been in a distant land to me.

I want to read your reflections because you too live in a distant land—the land of your novel or stories or memoir—and reading your work gives me an opportunity to travel to places unknown.

Well-crafted reflections can help me understand those unknown places all the more.

OMNISCIENT REFLECTION

Narrative reflection *without* a first-person protagonist's voice isn't used as often in reasonably current fiction as it once was. After Tolstoy's "Happy families are all alike; every unhappy family is unhappy in its own way" or Jane Austen's "It is a truth universally acknowledged, that a single man in possession of a good fortune must be in want of a wife" or Dickens's direct addresses to the reader, omniscience became a term more often denoting a disembodied external narrator who could enter the minds of many characters and describe their thoughts and actions rather than an all-knowing, godlike interpreter. Omniscient narrators became much less likely to comment on the story as it unfolded. Authors (except a few quirky ruminators and postmodern footnote extravagants) became uneasy with the idea of third-person narrators who make grand or even humble pronouncements. Our current sense of reality seems to be suspicious of a know-it-all narrator whose face we never see.

In 1919, Sherwood Anderson retained an old-fashioned omniscience, though much else about the novel *Winesburg, Ohio* was new. This narrator intervened on occasion, interrupting the narration with commentary or gentle guidance before plunging back into the story. In "Hands," the narrator says,

> The story of Wing Biddlebaum's hands is worth a book in itself. Sympathetically set forth it would tap many strange, beautiful qualities in obscure men. It is a job for a poet … Let us look briefly into the story of the hands. Perhaps our talking of them will arouse the poet who will tell the hidden wonder story of the influence for which the hands were but fluttering pennants of promise.

A few paragraphs later the reflective narrator criticizes himself: "And yet that is but crudely stated. It needs the poet there." This reflective narrator who insists on intruding on the story strikes a pose—that of both omniscience and self-deprecating modesty. "It requires a poet, it is crudely stated." This narrator separates himself from the mythical poet who, he tells us, should be the one to tell the tale. Here's a reflective narrator who is playing with the idea of narrator, reflecting, you might say, on the idea of storytelling. And that is a very postmodern idea!

For those who are writing historical fiction or period pieces, this sort of "old-fashioned" narrative reflection might serve you well if you wish to intentionally mimic the style of an earlier time. In practice, an omniscient reflective narrator is basically the same as a first-person reflective narrator except the narrator is a disembodied voice, *not* a character in the story. Yet the narrator sees and understands all.

Sometimes an omniscient reflective narrator can be used briefly as a device to begin a story before introducing or sliding into the mind of the protagonist, and it often only lasts for the first paragraph or two. John Cheever, in a story called "The Golden Age," begins with such a device. The narrator uses the first-person plural, we, to begin the tale of an American family staying in a castle in Europe (ellipses mine):

> Our ideas of castles, formed in childhood, are inflexible, and why try to reform them? ... Nothing is inconsequential here. It is thrilling to drink Martinis on the battlements, it is thrilling to bathe in the fountain, it is even thrilling to climb down the stairs into the village after supper and buy a box of matches. The drawbridge is down, the double doors are open, and early one morning we see a family crossing the moat, carrying the paraphernalia of a picnic. They are Americans. Nothing they can do will quite

conceal the touching ridiculousness, the clumsiness of the traveler.

This omniscient reflective narrator sets the context for us, a larger context perhaps than the characters might know themselves. He is paternal in his omniscience—he invites us to look at the characters from a condescending distance—at their American ridiculousness, which, no matter how absurd we too might seem when we travel abroad, we share with him for the moment. Thus he creates both intimacy and distance with his reader.

Cheever quickly shifts to ordinary summary from omniscient reflection and finally moves into the scene as we enter the minds of his characters—the glow of the television in a bar seems sad to these Americans. From that point on, the story proceeds by scene and summary.

In past decades there's been a resurgence of omniscient reflective narrators in the works of some well-known writers including Lemony Snicket and Philip Pullman (in young adult novels) and literary authors such as Salman Rushdie, Zadie Smith, Jonathan Franzen, Don DeLillo, David Foster Wallace, and others. Often these omniscient reflective narrators take an ironic tone—a sort of winking at the reader to say, "We know this is old-fashioned; it's a game we're playing." It's a game you can play if you care to, but you'll need to know your antecedents first, which means studying nineteenth-century omniscient reflective narrators to familiarize yourself with their diction, syntax, and general style in order to adapt them for your own purposes. If you take a look at some of the nineteenth-century authors mentioned above—Dickens, Tolstoy, Austen—you should get a good sense of the sort of omniscient reflective pronouncements they make and the language with which they make them.

RETROSPECTIVE REFLECTION

Much more often than omniscient reflection, contemporary writers use a *retrospective* reflective voice—an older narrator looking back on earlier days in her own life. Whether in fiction or memoir, this sort of reflection accompanies scenes and other forms of summary because the retrospective narrator is in a position to better understand the meaning of events lived through as a child or youth. That distance between older, wiser narrator and younger self as character is an essential part of a retrospective story or memoir. It allows the reader to follow the narrator or character's journey to a wiser self, and the older character or narrator's reflection is the means by which we comprehend *the meaning* of events in the life of the younger self.

Though the retrospective narrator is more common in creative nonfiction, fiction also has reflective retrospective narrators. For example, in Ralph Ellison's classic novel *Invisible Man*, the older, wiser reflective voice precedes the younger point of view:

> I am an invisible man. No, I am not a spook like those who haunted Edgar Allan Poe; nor am I one of our Hollywood-movie ectoplasms. I am a man of substance, of flesh and bone, fiber and liquids—and I might even be said to possess a mind. I am invisible, understand, simply because people refuse to see me.

Ellison's older narrator relays a scene in which he, as a young high school valedictorian, is supposed to give his graduation speech to his segregated city's (this is the 1940s and Ellison is African-American) leading white citizens at a hotel. But first he's forced to perform in a humiliating and bloody "Battle Royal" with other young black men for the drunken white men's entertainment. After he's allowed to give his speech and awarded a briefcase, he speaks in the voice (in a scene) of the clueless young man who thinks of himself as a potential Booker T. Washington: "I was so moved that I could hardly express my thanks. A rope of bloody saliva ... drooled upon the leather and I wiped it quickly away. I felt an importance that I had never dreamed."

The reader (because of the older, retrospective narrator's earlier reflections) knows that this "importance" is illusory even if the young protagonist doesn't, despite what he's just been through. The entire novel can be seen as the narrator's journey from innocence to painful knowledge—his coming to understand his position as a black man in 1940s America. Without this narrative layering complete with adult reflection, Ellison would either be relaying the story of a naïf or conversely giving us the viewpoint of an enlightened but disillusioned man without our seeing the steps along the way that brought him to this position of pained cynicism. Without the scenes and summaries of his innocence, the voice of wisdom would have much less power. And without the older reflective voice, the reader wouldn't understand the ultimate effect of the narrator's experiences on him. We'd have no wiser voice to guide us.

If you are writing fiction or creative nonfiction with a retrospective narrator who reflects on his younger self, there are techniques you can use to make your reflection effective.

First, you must define the differences between the narrator's older and younger selves. Ask yourself, is the younger narrator/character: Naïve? Energetic? Hopeful? Full of illusions? Given to excesses? Does she drink too much? Jump from relationship to relationship? Submissive with authority?Impoverished? Abused? Happy-go-lucky? Whatever the nature of the younger narrator/character, you need to pin it down.

Now define this younger person's situation in terms of geography, housing, family, school, work, etc.

Who is the adult or older narrator now? Ask the same questions of your "wiser" narrator.

Next ask yourself, how does the adult narrator feel about this younger self? Sympathetic? Cynical? Patient? Angry? Remorseful? Resentful? Judgmental? Jealous? Curious? Detached? It's up to you to find the right adjective, but if the answer is "detached" that means there is a broken connection between the narrator's younger and older self and this must be righted. You'll have to find a way to connect the older narrator to his or her younger self or the retrospective reflection won't have depth and power. One way to overcome detachment is to figure out the motives of the younger person—*why* was she that silly or he that cruel? Sometimes when we understand our character's motives we gain sympathy for them and the reader does too.

If you answered that your reflective narrator feels very judgmental toward her younger self, this too can spoil the experience for your reader. I had just this problem in writing my first memoir *Fault Line*. In it I told the story of a brilliant young man I'd met and become involved with when I was sixteen, a high school kid, and he was a junior on a scholarship at Harvard. Over many years or so we had a tortured relationship and I was responsible for a lot of the torturing. We'd been out of touch for many years when I learned that his decomposed body had been discovered in Wyoming. By that point he lived out of his car. After his death his car was located and in it was found a small box of his belongings, including a photo of us from 1970 that he'd carried for twenty-five years. I felt such guilt about the course of our relationship and my possible role in his decline that the first draft of my memoir created a version of myself that everyone I showed the draft to hated. It wasn't until I included a retrospective reflective narrator, myself as a settled adult—wife, mother, writer, college professor—that I was able to balance the overwhelmingly negative presentation of my much younger self that resulted from my feelings of guilt.

The opposite situation—your reflective older narrator being *too* sympathetic to a younger self—can cause just as many problems. If your narrator reflects on his earlier self in too rosy a light, honesty can be sacrificed, leading to the reader losing confidence, trust, and ultimately interest in the narrator and story. Ask yourself, are you letting your narrator off the hook? Have you been completely honest in your assessment of the narrator both younger and older? Reflection along the order of "boys will be boys" will not have much impact on a reader.

Finally, ask yourself what the adult narrator feels about her younger self in various situations that arise in your story. They may be conflicting emotions—that's okay, we are contradictory beings. What does the adult narrator feel if her younger self was victimized, if the younger self achieved, if the younger self made foolish choices—be specific, responding to scenes from your story. If an older Sally looked back at young Sally on her first day teaching kindergarten when she goes down the slide in her espadrilles and breaks her ankle, what would older Sally think about it? Would she want to warn her or laugh at her?

You'll be able to write your adult narrator's response to his younger self once you know fully who he is as a person.

REFLECTIVE DIGRESSIONS—FROM THE PERSONAL TO INFORMATIONAL OR UNIVERSAL

Reflection, in both fiction and creative nonfiction, can also mean an opportunity to travel away from the main currents of the story or essay, to express knowledge or opinions on even tangentially related topics. When I was in junior high and bored in class, I used to play a silent game I called fishing. I would let my mind roam and then reel in, tracing back the path of mental associations. Associative or digressive reflection is much like the first part of the game, casting out your net or line to see what you might bring up from the depths.

Reflection that "digresses" from the personal to the historical or informational can make a narrative both more layered and more thought provoking. In Louise Erdrich's nonfiction book about being a mother, *The Blue Jay's Dance*, she moves from the utterly personal—her fantasies about her yet-to-be-born child—to the biological, historic, philosophical, then back to the personal once again:

> ... because I am a mammal I am condemned to give birth
> through the lower part of my body while flowers, though
> brainless, have the wisdom to shoot straight upward in a
> pure green rush from unpromising seeds.

Erdrich goes on to tell us how she's no hero, afraid of needles and blood, but then she moves away from these details about herself to ask why women giving birth aren't valorized like Socrates with his cup of hemlock. She blames it on a tradition begun with Genesis, in which pain in childbirth is a punishment for Eve's curiosity:

> Over all of the millennia that women have endured and
> suffered and died during childbirth, we have no one sto-
> ry that comes down to us with a attendant reverence ...
> War heroes routinely receive medals for killing and de-
> fending. Why don't women routinely receive medals for
> giving birth?

Erdrich, because she is primarily writing a personal book, returns quickly to her individual experience, summarizing her mother's labor during her own birth. But her reflections about the history of childbirth have made their point and enlarged her essay beyond the strictly personal. There are those reflective writers such as Annie Dillard, whose personal experience is a jumping-off point, not just for the general or the universal but for the cosmic. She's interested in a much greater level of abstraction than is Erdrich. Following the excerpt from *Pilgrim at Tinker Creek* that appears in Section I, she takes off from the experience of patting a puppy at a gas station to reflect on the nature of consciousness, going so far as to quote a scholar on the subject. While Erdrich drifts between the poles of her experiences and her ruminations, Dillard uses her personal experience to illustrate and expand her philosophical stance about nature, time, being. She uses the concrete as a ladder to great abstractions. Yet when she's gone too far for you, she comes back to the most precise observations of the world around her. With less—but not a whole deal less—moralizing, she is the direct descendent of Thoreau.

But not all digressive reflection has to be of such a high order of abstraction. You might want to add digressive reflection to your work as a means of adding interest—maybe not to the extent that Tolstoy does in giving the history of Napoleon's invasion of Russia in *War and Peace,* but perhaps to the extent that Chris Bohjalian does in his novel *Water Witches* (ellipses mine):

> In shape, in size, in sheer accessibility, there may be no more perfect mountain in this world than Mount Republic. It is not tall, though it is one of the higher mountains in Vermont ... Its mold was a giant teacup, pressed firmly into the molten mud that once was once this planet, and then removed when the mud had cooled and the mountain was made.

This sort of digressive reflection—the narrator judges the perfection of a certain mountain and then tells you something about its geological history before he enters into a scene in which he is riding a chairlift with a ski company executive—simply serves to bring the reader deeper into the setting of the story. But the digression only lasts for a paragraph before the author starts to bring the narrative elements back into play. The author is careful not to interrupt his novel for too long. Certainly there are authors whose digressive reflection goes on much longer; they need very strong voices to interrupt their narrative momentum at great length without the reader losing interest or forgetting where the story was going.

REFLECTION AND HUMOR

Reflection, of course, can have less grand ambitions than the writers I've excerpted above, such as Dillard or Erdrich or Anderson. It can be humorous and its purpose can be to entertain. Irony, absurdity, exaggeration, odd juxtapositions, and sarcasm stand many writers from Mark Twain to David Sedaris in good stead. Scenes offer opportunities for humor through behavior and dialogue. Summary gives a writer the opportunity to express humor through reflection, apart from actions or speech.

In *A Primate's Memoir,* the biologist Robert Sapolsky surprises us with a humorous one-two punch: "I joined the baboon troop during my twenty-first year. I had never planned to become a savanna baboon when I grew up; instead, I had always assumed I would become a mountain gorilla." It's unusual, to say the least, to find an American male who considers himself a savanna baboon, but even more surprising to learn that as a youth he'd expected to become a gorilla.

Susan Orlean, in her essay "Show Dog," withholds information for comic effect:

> If I were a bitch, I'd be in love with Biff Truesdale. Biff is perfect. He's friendly, good looking, rich, famous, and in excellent physical condition. He almost never drools. He's not afraid of commitment. He wants children—actually, he already has children and wants a lot more ... What Biff likes most is food and sex. This makes him sound

boorish, which he is not—he's just elemental. Food he likes even better than sex. His favorite things to eat are cookies, mints, and hotel soap, but he will eat just about anything.

Despite the title, and the fact that Orlean gives hints along the way, such as Biff eating hotel soap, we're still surprised to learn that Biff is a boxer, a show dog. The effect is playful, though the language is straightforward. It would be near impossible to get this effect in a scene.

Bill Bryson, in *In a Sunburned Country*, his travel book on Australia, relies on the simplest mode of humor, the put-down:

> It's possible I suppose, to construct hypothetical circumstances in which you would be pleased to find yourself, at the end of a long day, in Macksville, New South Wales—perhaps something to do with rising sea levels that left it as the only place on earth not under water, or maybe some disfiguring universal contagion from which it alone remained unscathed.

Bryson accomplishes his put-down of this particular place by the extremity and absurdity of his examples. But he doesn't put down his reader—he implies that we are all buddies here and that we share his assumptions and his wit. Again, this sort of commentary would sound awkward if voiced in dialogue in a scene.

In *Me Talk Pretty One Day*, David Sedaris employs a variety of complex techniques in his humorous reflection:

> ... the French would never like us, and that's confusing to an American raised to believe that the citizens of Europe should be grateful for all the wonderful things we've done. Things like movies that stereotype the people of France as boors and petty snobs, and little remarks such as "We saved your ass in World War II." Every day we're told that

> we live in the greatest country on earth ... Having grown
> up with this in our ears, it's startling to realize that other
> countries have nationalistic slogans of their own, none of
> which are "We're number two."

Sedaris goes on to discuss how he doesn't care if the French
hate us as long as he can buy taxidermied kittens there, and he
jokes that the only reason to leave your native country is to go
shopping. Sedaris manages to be critical of us as Americans—
and *us* is an important word here, because if he were critical of
readers and didn't include himself, we'd become annoyed and
resentful rather than laugh. He is mildly self-critical of his own
values (shopping being the only reason to travel), he takes a
swipe at the French who sell taxidermied kittens, and he uses
his desire for those kittens as a reflection of his own twisted
mind. Much is accomplished in this short excerpt that couldn't
occur in a scene.

Aside from the ridiculous names, in Eudora Welty's classic of
the unreliable narrator story "Why I Live at the P.O.," the humor
comes from the distance between what the narrator tells and
what the reader understands:

> I was getting along fine with Mama, Papa-Daddy and
> uncle Rondo until my sister Stella-Rondo just separated
> from her husband came back home again. Mr. Whitaker!
> Of course I went with Mr. Whitaker first, when he first
> appeared here in China Grove, taking "Pose Yourself"
> photos, and Stella-Rondo broke us up. Told him I was
> one-sided. Bigger on one side than the other, which is a
> deliberate calculated falsehood: I'm the same.

These humorous reflective techniques—withholding information,
exaggeration, poking fun at oneself, poking fun at others, playful language, reversing expectations, unreliable narrators—to

some degree require a natural humorous bent on the part of the writer. Humor is probably the hardest thing to teach, and there are many who believe it cannot be taught. Even those who can recognize humor in others' writing often can't find the humor in their own (I sadly count myself among this group). And many of these methods—unreliable reflective narrators or characters, for instance—can be tragic rather than humorous in certain situations. Imagine, for instance, a child who mistakenly interprets the actions of adults to their detriment, as Briony does in Ian McEwan's *Atonement*. (That novel happens to be written in a close third-person rather than a first-person point of view.) This unreliable point of view is tragic in McEwan's novel and funny in Eudora Welty's story "Why I Live at the P.O." Surely the consequences of the error make the difference between tragedy and humor here; if you wish to find the humor in an unreliable narrator or point of view you can't have the results of that narrator's misapprehensions end in the destruction of a love affair or the death of a soldier. The consequences must be as light as the setup.

Nonetheless, you can play around with these techniques, looking for opportunities for withholding information to humorous effect as Susan Orlean does, finding places to surprise your reader like Sapolsky, making fun of your own or your narrator's weaknesses like Sedaris, searching for the absurdity in everyday situations. Even in discussing humor I have to come back to the idea of intention, however. You must decide if your piece is going to be light in tone, a piece of entertainment, or basically serious with a few touches of irony, a few laughs. What won't work is if you keep wavering between intentions—using your characters for humorous effect and then expecting people to be moved by their loves and losses. Sure, there are a few masters who have the ability to treat dead serious situations humorously, like Joseph Heller in *Catch-22* or David Sedaris in some of his more serious pieces, such as ones about his mother's death, or Lorrie

Moore in her funny and sad novel *Anagrams,* for instance. But it's a very hard balancing act to pull off and those who do it well are few and far between. My advice is to be fully aware of your own intent and stay consistent within that intent. If your aim is to entertain more than it is to illuminate, go ahead and make use of such humorous reflective techniques as narrative exaggeration. If your intention is primarily literary, look for the irony and the absurdity in your story and let it shine without allowing it overwhelm the story or the characters.

AMOUNT OF REFLECTION

What is the right amount of omniscient, personal, or digressive reflection? Reflection, like flashbacks, slows the action. It interrupts the narrative's forward movement. So any reflection you add to your story must be worth the loss of momentum, in terms of adding insight or interest for the reader. Of course, if you're writing a meditative rather than a narrative essay, which might move by association rather than a chronology of action, the piece will depend on reflection rather than plot, so a lot of reflection (as long as it is relevant and well written) will not be a problem. But if you are writing anything that is driven by story, just be aware that your reflection must consistently *add* rather than take away from the impact of the overall piece. If you are writing a story and there is more reflection than action, you've certainly got too much of a good thing. (Okay, there are always exceptions to all rules. Not all stories are plot driven either. But let's assume you are writing a story with a plot.) You don't want your narrator stopping to comment on the action and characters at such length that your reader has forgotten what's going on in the story by the time you get back to it. It's a balancing act, one that may require some trial and error on your part.

Chapter 8

MORE TOOLS OF THE SUMMARY TRADE

DETAIL

Much of what I've written about the use of detail in scene in Section I holds true for summary. Detail can make summary as vivid as scenes, and the details you use can have significant and symbolic weight as well as literal meaning. Selecting your details carefully is important no matter how you are using summary—for background information, compressing time, developing characters, etc.

In his story "Artemis, the Honest Well Digger," John Cheever's summarizing narrator not only tells us what Artemis thinks and feels, but he is free to comment on related or even seemingly unrelated aspects of life. Yet he is never general. Look at the details:

> Artemis loved the healing sound of rain—the sound of all running water—brooks, gutters, spouts, falls, and taps. In the spring he would drive one hundred miles to hear the cataract at the Wakusha Reservoir. This was not so surprising because he was a well driller and water was his profession, his livelihood, as well as his passion. Water, he thought, was at the root of civilizations ... To get the facts out of the way: Artemis drilled with an old Smith &

> Mathewson chain-concussion rig that struck the planet
> sixty blows a minute ...

Artemis's fascination with water is made explicit via details, and the details further our understanding of Artemis's character—his passion for water. The narrator then goes on to tell us where he lived and how many flags Artemis's mother had on her house. Whatever Cheever tells us works toward deepening themes or revealing character. For example, the narrator seemingly veers off on a tangent all his own about the displaying of flags on private property, noting that poor people, who have garnered less of their country's riches, seem the most patriotic. But the fact that Artemis's mother displays flags isn't just some quirky detail to characterize Artemis's background or his home. The question of patriotism mentioned here is later echoed when Artemis becomes involved with a Russian woman while on vacation in Russia and is called in to report to the State Department. Each detail, even when summarized, contributes to the whole story.

When possible, allow your detail to do more than one job. Ask yourself if the details you use in your summaries serve to reveal character or further themes. For example, do you want the bug on the wall to be a spider or a roach? What associations do each of these bugs carry? If you're writing about a character who tends to weave little webs of deceit in her gossip, then by all means, choose the spider! If you're writing about a pathologically shy man who scuttles about hiding from other people, you might want to choose the roach. Of course, if you're writing creative nonfiction and you remember specifically that it was a spider, then it's a spider. The point here is that the details you use in your summaries shouldn't be random. They add to the overall effect.

Another excerpt from Tobias Wolff's *This Boy's Life* proves that summary can be as vivid as any scene (ellipses mine):

> It was 1955 and we were driving from Florida to Utah,
> to get away from a man my mother was afraid of and
> to get rich on uranium. We were going to change our
> luck … We drove through Georgia, Alabama, Tennessee,
> Kentucky, stopping to cool the engine in towns where
> people moved with arthritic slowness and spoke in thick,
> strangled tongues … At night we slept in boggy rooms
> where headlight beams crawled up and down the walls
> and mosquitoes sang in our ears, incessant as the tires
> whining on the highway outside.

In Wolff's summary, you can practically hear the whining mosquitoes in your own ears.

This summary from John Updike's story "The Persistence of Desire" begins in a nonspecified time, with the character Clyde thinking about how he always admired certain qualities in a former lover. And at first the qualities and actions that he remembers are described rather generally. Though still in summary, Updike begins to add the kind of detail that makes a summary as memorable as a scene (ellipses mine):

> He had always admired this competence in her, her au-
> thority in the world peripheral to the world of love in which
> she was so servile … she could outface waitresses and …
> would bluff her mother when this vicious woman unex-
> pectedly entered the screened porch where they were
> supposed to be playing cribbage. Potted elephant plants
> sat in the corners like faithful dwarfs; robins had built a
> nest in the lilac outside, inches from the screen. It had
> been taken as an omen, a blessing, when one evening
> their being on the glider no longer distressed the birds.

Not only does Updike put elephant plants into this summary, but he uses a simile—they sat like faithful dwarfs! There were robins inches from the screen and they were no longer afraid of the humans on the glider (these two must have been doing a lot of glider sitting!). Moreover, these robins became a blessing for the young lovers. As a side note, you might wonder why Updike uses the passive voice— "It had been taken as an omen … " rather than the more active "we took it as an omen … " Normally we're told to use the active voice. But in this case the syntax matches the protagonist's emotional distance. As you read the story you come to see that this narrator is unable to extend compassion or even an acknowledgement of his former lover's existence as a human separate from his own needs. Back to the example, though—Updike's details bring the summary to vibrant life.

Isabel Allende, in her novel *Of Love and Shadows*, provides another example of specific detail enlivening a background summary and even creating narrative tension:

> From Monday to Friday the children walked to school, a half hour's rapid walk. When it was cold, the mother gave each child a stone heated in the fire to put in a pocket to keep their hands warm. She also gave them a piece of bread and two sugar lumps. Earlier, when milk was still being served at school, they used the sugar to sweeten it, but for several years now they had sucked the lumps like caramels during recess.

Imagine this summarized as: "The children walked to school. Their mother gave them hand warmers and food to take with them." From both versions we understand that the mother cared for her children. But in Allende's version, we know that the mother went to the trouble of heating stones in a fire to warm their hands. This is a woman who can't run to the corner store to buy chemical hand warmers—her life is more basic, less modern. We also know that for some reason the school no longer provides milk for the children. Some change has taken place. And the kids suck on the sugar lumps "like caramels." Their mother has enough to give them sugar, but not enough to provide candy. A great deal more information has been offered in Allende's detailed version and it isn't simply factual. The school's inability to provide now what it could provide earlier brings tension into the summary. The summary has been enlivened by detail but it has also been made more complex, more dramatic.

TECHNIQUES FOR MAKING DETAILS COUNT IN SUMMARY

- Don't stick to the obvious, overly familiar detail in your summary descriptions. Make them fresh and vivid. Wolff doesn't say that headlights *shone* into the room; he has them *crawl up and down the walls*, which plays off the bugs tormenting Wolff and his mother already. You don't want to write about a *hunched old lady* or *verdant landscapes*. These details are devalued by their overuse. If your old lady has the posture of a wilting flower, you've made her vivid and your summary enlivened.

- Besides giving concrete information, do your details advance theme? Wolff says that they left to get away from a man *his mother was afraid of*. If he'd said only that they left, or even left to get away from a man, he wouldn't have established the same element of danger that will become an important aspect of this memoir, nor would he have been able to use his mother's past bad choices about men to foreshadow themes to come.

- To reveal character through summary detail in your own work, choose features of behavior or appearance that expose a character's inner life. Compare "She often saw a middle-aged man in a business suit walking down the sidewalk" to "She often saw a middle-aged man in a business suit walking down the sidewalk being careful not to step on any cracks." What do you know about the second man that you didn't know about the first? What details of appearance and behavior can you give your own characters to expose their idiosyncrasies, hopes, or fears?

- Make your summary details create tension or drama when possible. Even the man walking down the sidewalk being careful to not step on cracks creates tension. We want to know what his problem is, and maybe what will happen if he steps on a crack by accident. Tension is created when a detail raises an unanswered question.

NARRATIVE LAYERING

I mentioned this topic in the chapter on retrospective reflection, above. It's worth looking at a bit further, however. Narrative layering refers to a first-person work in which the narrator is seen at either a younger and older age, or from a more naïve as well as a more experienced perspective. There is a tension inherent in the inclusion of both these points of view—one that has no idea what's going on and one that is able to interpret events for the reader. Narrative layering is of particular importance in pieces or books that inhabit the mind of a narrator whose age changes over the course of the work. Thus it frequently appears in memoirs. But it is also useful in works in which the narrator or a point of view character changes *in understanding,* as shown in Ralph Ellison's novel *Invisible Man.* Sometimes the changes in age or wisdom aren't incorporated as part of the ongoing story line. Instead, the layered narrative includes occasional interjections by an older narrator while the main story is of the younger self. In other words, there doesn't have to be a retrospective reflective frame, as with *Invisible Man*. We don't have to see the narrator looking back on life from a specific vantage point in which we know the details of his older situation. How much space is given to the younger/more innocent vs. the older/wiser narrator depends on the tastes of the author. A book like Frank McCourt's *Angela's Ashes* is very subtle in its use of adult interjections though they exist.

In the above excerpt from *This Boy's Life* and through much of that memoir, Wolff vacillates between various forms of narrative distance in his summaries. He uses the child's simple language in the assertion about his mother and his trip across country: "We were going to change our luck." Of course the adult Tobias Wolff knows (as does the reader) that their luck won't change for the better. Later he uses adult language and the wisdom of the adult self when he says, "I was caught up in my mother's freedom, her delight in her freedom, her dream of transformation."

So we get, in this summary, along with the vividness of scene created by sensory detail, the opportunity to view the world through the eyes of the ten-year-old boy that Wolff was, with all his hope and naiveté, as well as to see world through the eyes of the adult Wolff who will comment on the action, interpret for us, and even jump forward in time to compare something happening to young Toby with something that happened later to the adult Wolff (service in Vietnam, for instance). Scene alone would not offer up such layered information, nor would a single-age narrator.

If you are writing a work of fiction or a memoir from a first-person point of view, you may well want to explore the possibilities of layering your narrative so your summaries can reveal the way your narrator sees the world at different ages and stages of maturity. You should find the techniques listed in the retrospective reflection chapter helpful. But remember that each time you interject an older or wiser perspective, you are interrupting the narrative flow. What would make an interjection or juxtaposed perspective worthwhile? It must further the reader's understanding of characters and situations in an *essential* way. Consider if that older or wiser view allows the reader to absorb changes taking place in the younger or more innocent narrator. Ask yourself if there is a better place for inserting the information that the older narrator will provide. Does it need to go right here in the midst of the younger person's story? Why? If you have a strong rationale for interjecting, go for it.

TONE AND MOOD

Tone refers to the narrator's attitude toward the material; mood is the emotional state engendered in the reader by the material. Summaries are often the place where tone and mood get established, particularly when scenes are allowed to unfold without much interior commentary within characters.

The tone of a piece can be urgent, dismissive, judgmental, ironic, sentimental, mocking, harsh, alarmed, sympathetic, and any other number of adjectives that describe and qualify experience. Think of what we mean when we say "I don't like your tone." We are reacting to subtle or not so subtle cues that come from shadings in the volume, speed, and cast of the voice. A big brother could tell his bored little brother "Go fly a kite," with a tone of enthusiasm and encouragement, or he could say, "Go fly a kite" and mean "get lost." As humans going about our daily lives we've become attuned to picking up meaning from the tone of voice of our family members, teachers, bosses, doctors, salespeople, employees, friends, and children. In writing, we can't convey tone by the softness or loudness or sharpness of an actual, audible voice. So we have to impart tone via the situation.

With characters, we can usually figure out tone through our understanding of what has happened or is happening in the situation they find themselves in and in the relationship between them if it is already established. With the narrator, it's sometimes a bit more difficult, although once you've established a narrator's tone you can generally assume that it will remain consistent throughout the work. If it doesn't there's a problem in the writing or the narrator wants you to notice the tone shift for a reason. Let's look at some published examples of narrative tone.

It's not very difficult to determine Jamaica Kincaid's tone in her book-length nonfiction essay, *A Small Place:*

> An ugly thing, that is what you are when you become a tourist, an ugly, empty thing, a stupid thing, a piece of rubbish pausing here and there to gaze at this and taste that, it will never occur to you that the people who inhabit the place in which you have just paused cannot stand you, that behind their closed doors they laugh at your strangeness ... you have bad manners (it is their custom to eat their food with their hands; you try eating their way, you look silly; you try eating the way you always eat, you look silly) ...

The narrator's tone here is judgmental and dismissive. The piece is written in second person, addressed directly to the reader, creating a *mood* of unease and perhaps even indignation in the reader. This judgment is a rhetorical device—the narrator tells the reader that she is ugly and laughable to the natives whom the reader, when a tourist, might be guilty of judging equally ugly or laughable. The tone forces the reader to examine her own prejudices and assumptions, but when this harsh tone is addressed to "you" there's a danger of making readers turn away.

Thomas Lynch, in his memoir about being a funeral director, *The Undertaking,* adopts a pragmatic and sometimes ironic tone. Where people die is all the same to the man who handles the dead and, as the excerpt goes on to explain, to the dead themselves:

> They die around the clock here, without apparent preference for a day of the week, month of the year; there is no clear favorite in the way of season. Nor does the alignment of the stars, fullness of moon, or liturgical calendar have very much to do with it. The whereabouts are neither here nor there. They go off upright or horizontally in Chevrolets and nursing homes, in bathtubs, on the interstates, in ERs, ORs, BMWs.

Lynch's decidedly ungloomy, nonfunereal tone permits us to take a clear-eyed look at a rather taboo subject.

Lorrie Moore's narrator, in her short story "People Like That Are the Only People Here," is laughing in the dark (ellipses mine):

> A start: the Mother finds a blood clot in the Baby's diaper. What is the story? Who put this here? It is big and bright with a broken, khaki-colored vein in it. ... what is this thing, startling against the white diaper, like a tiny mouse packed in snow? Perhaps it belongs to someone else. Perhaps it is something menstrual, something belonging to the Mother or to the Babysitter, something the Baby has found in a wastebasket and for his own demented baby reasons stowed away here. (Babies—they're crazy! What can you do?)

The situation is horrible—a baby with a serious, life-threatening health problem. The tone is jokey but definitely not light. (What can you do, indeed?) The mood engendered is one of fear and instant sympathy for this mother's near hysteria that takes the form of black humor.

Louise Erdrich's tone, in the novel *Tracks*, is mythical and mysterious: "The first time she drowned in the cold and glassy waters of Lake Turcot, Fleur Pillager was only a girl." Readers are forced to wonder what unfamiliar realm they have entered in which a young girl can drown more than once. The mood is one of suspension of disbelief.

F. Scott Fitzgerald, in *The Great Gatsby*, uses a tone, at least in this section of the novel, that is mythic and poetic:

> About halfway between West Egg and New York the motor-road hastily joins the railroad and runs beside it for a quarter of a mile so as to shrink away from a certain desolate area of land. This is a valley of ashes—a fantastic farm where ashes grow like wheat into ridges and hills and grotesque gardens, where ashes take the forms of houses and chimneys and rising smoke and finally, with a transcendent effort, of men who move dimly and already crumbling through the powdery air.

We have entered the world of metaphor and simile in a "desolate" and "grotesque" valley of ashes in which ashes grow like wheat on a farm and take the shapes of houses and crumbling ash men. The mood is one of horror—even the road seems to shrink away from this terrible place.

Pam Houston, in her short story "How to Talk to a Hunter," uses the second person as a means of distancing the narrator from herself. The tone is both ironic and anguished:

> The hunter will talk about spring in Hawaii, summer in Alaska. The man who says he was always better at math will form the sentences so carefully it will be impossible to tell if you are included in these plans. When he asks you if you would like to open a small guest ranch way out in the country, understand that this is a rhetorical question.

David Foster Wallace, in his essay "Consider the Lobster," strikes a tone of relentless questioning—of the broader culture and of himself. At the heart of the essay is an ethical dilemma, and he wants to be on the right side without seeming sentimental:

> So then here is a question that's all but unavoidable at the World's Largest Lobster Cooker, and may arise in the kitchens across the United States: Is it all right to boil a sentient creature alive just for our gustatory pleasure? A related set of concerns: Is the previous question irksomely PC or sentimental? What does "all right" even mean in this context? Is it all just a matter of personal choice?

Wallace is obviously disturbed by the pain inflicted on lobsters though he knows that there are those who will judge him as a bleeding heart. He's trying to have it both ways—address what he perceives as horror and excuse himself from being "too PC." His tone is a complex mixture of impassioned judgment and ironic detachment. The mood engendered, in this lobster-eating reader anyway, is one of queasy guilt.

Before you develop mastery over narrative tone to the extent that you can experiment with it, it helps to become aware of tone in the works of other writers and start seeing how you have, perhaps unintentionally, applied tone in your own writing. Sometimes I see students use a joking or ironic voice on material that is very painful for them to write, as though they can keep from feeling by making light of it. Sure, Lorrie Moore uses humor very well in her story excerpted above, but she always lets us see the fear underneath the jokes. Ask yourself if you are using irony or humor as a way to avoid emotion. Other times, inexperienced writers use an overly earnest or overly poetic tone that demands readers acknowledge that this is a Very Serious Subject or the writer is a Very Creative Person. But we readers don't like to be forced—we want the tone to fit the material subtly and organically. Again, when you examine use of tone in your own writing, make sure you aren't trying to stack the deck or force your audience. One of your purposes in choosing a particular tone is to create a mood in your reader, and the mood will be spoiled if the tone detracts from or overwhelms the material.

LANGUAGE

Much of my commentary on the use of language in scenes holds true for language in summary. Syntax, diction, metaphor, and simile in summary work much the way they do in scenes. Here are a few notes on diction in summaries.

Diction (word choice) and syntax (sentence structure) can help set the tone of a summary. Just as in dialogue, if the narration is meant to be informal and conversational, the writer will choose ordinary words that one would hear in conversation, as in this excerpt from Sandra Cisneros's *The House on Mango Street*:

> We didn't always live on Mango Street. Before that we lived on Loomis on the third floor, and before that we lived on Keeler. Before Keeler it was Paulina, and before that I can't remember. But what I remember most is moving a lot.

The repetition of "before that" has an everyday quality, as does the informal phrase "a lot." In this case we have a child narrator, but such informality can exist with adult narrators or characters as well.

When an author uses abstract, Latinate words in the narration, the tone is more formal and suggests an insistence on more complex ideas. This excerpt comes from Mark Doty's memoir *Dog Years*:

> Here is an ancient problem. Before the creation of the world, God was alone, but He (I use the pronoun merely for convenience since there is no adequate one) was also

omnipresent. In order to assuage His loneliness by creating a world that was not Himself, there had to be some
place in which He did not exist. He did this, the Kabbalists
say, by "withdrawing from some region of Himself."

Ancient, creation, pronoun, convenience, adequate, omnipresent, assuage—though several of these words contain only two
syllables and are not particularly complex in and of themselves,
together they set a tone of erudition, of philosophical complexity.
The word choice establishes the attitude of the narration.

Your choice of formal or informal diction in summaries
will help establish the tone and mood you want in your work,
as will simple or complex syntax. In first-person narratives, a
shift from simple to more complex language over the course of
a story can demonstrate a change in the narrator's age and/or
sophistication.

Symbolic language—metaphor and similes—is as useful in
summaries as it is in scenes as long as it is fresh and not cliché.
And, as mentioned in Section I, your metaphors and similes must
suit the material they are illustrating.

Chapter 9

THE SINS OF SUMMARY

THE SIN OF UNNECESSARY EXPOSITION

When is exposition necessary and when is it not? Any exposition that tells what is already being shown in a scene is definitely unnecessary. Exposition that duplicates what is spoken in dialogue is particularly onerous, as in this example:

"Ow, I hit my thumb with the hammer!" Jack said, throwing the hammer on the floor. Jack had bashed his thumb with the hammer and he wasn't very happy about it.

Clearly, the dialogue and action have already shown what happened and how Jack felt about it, so the line of exposition following is wasted words. However, if the exposition stated that "Jack often bashed his thumb with hammers and doors and he'd even once stepped on his thumb while tying his shoe," the summary would be useful because it would reveal an oddity about Jack's character—either he is exceedingly clumsy or self-destructive.

Other unnecessary exposition occurs when details and facts are thrown in for their own sake without contributing to the overall work. If the writer gives us an entire genealogy of a character's family when the character is minor or if the story of his great-great-great-grandparents has no bearing on the central story, that would be unnecessary exposition.

Question the necessity of your expository summaries. Are you offering information in your exposition that can be eliminated because it is extraneous (like that family genealogy) or better shown through scenes? Try removing some of your exposition to see if anything has really been lost.

THE SIN OF MISPLACED SUMMARY

Misplaced summary occurs when a writer summarizes what really should be a scene. If you're reading a child the story of the Three Little Pigs and you simply summarize the scenes in which the Big Bad Wolf appears, skipping all that dialogue about huffing and puffing and blowing houses down by summarizing "The wolf showed up and destroyed the pigs' houses and ate a couple of them," the child will not be very satisfied. Likewise, if you are writing a memoir in which you run off to join the circus and only tell us that you met some pretty odd characters there and did some wild things, your reader will not be satisfied either. (For a terrific chapter on joining the circus, check out Chris Offutt's memoir *The Same River Twice*.) The reader needs scenes to have the experience of living through important events with the narrator or characters. If you summarize these, even if you enliven the summary with concrete details, the story or book will feel distanced and reported. Summaries have a lot of jobs to do, but bringing to life an important individual event isn't one of them.

Go back through your summaries and make sure that they don't contain a reported version of an event that requires evoking in scene. If it is a moment of revelation or major change in the life of the narrator or protagonist, it probably should be a scene, not summary.

THE SIN OF GENERALIZATIONS

All-encompassing statements about ethnicity, gender, age, education, and so on are usually insulting. (We all know to be wary when someone begins a sentence with "You people ... ") Even generalized praise, such as "Women are closer to the secret of life than men" or "The Irish have the gift of gab," is an insult, as it devalues the individuality of human beings within groups. Generalizations in summary are an affront to the reader, as they show that the writer is wasting the reader's time by not individualizing experience:

> Doris and Edward went on vacation in Santa Fe. They stayed at La Fonda hotel and ate a lot of New Mexican food. They enjoyed strolling the Plaza and visiting galleries.

This bland, empty narration reminds me of those awful massmailed Christmas letters (or e-mails) that come unbidden and single-spaced for page after page after page. See if you can identify any generalizations in your own summaries. Spend a little time with each one, asking yourself how you might transform the generalization into a richly descriptive portrayal. For example, take Doris and Edward's dully summarized New Mexican vacation and make it come alive:

> At the La Fonda (not *The* La Fonda, Doris kept saying, La means The), the décor was garishly festive with primary colors and primitive styles—painted on the windows, the carved headboards, in the shops eager to sell them painted tiles, pueblo pottery, turquoise and silver jewelry, and paintings of New Age Natives—thunderbird spirits with feathers and flowing blankets that they could

see in every gallery on the Plaza. Edward got indigestion
from the stuffed sopapillas and green chile stew.

THE SIN OF OPACITY OR TOO MUCH ABSTRACTION

In Delmore Shwartz's story "The World Is a Wedding," the
reflective narrator begins:

> In this our life there are no beginnings but only depar-
> tures entitled beginnings, wreathed in the formal emo-
> tions thought to be appropriate and often forced. Darkly
> rises each moment from the life which has been lived
> and which does not die, for each event lives in the heavy
> head forever, waiting to renew itself.

What is the difference between a *departure* and a *beginning*?
What *formal emotions* is he writing about? What is the *life that
does not die* and why does each moment rise from it *darkly*?
What does Schwartz mean when he says that *each event waits
to renew itself*? The level of abstraction here is so great that it's
very hard to figure out what the writer is getting at and therefore hard to become engaged with the material. The profound
has been replaced by the vague. As a general rule, and there are
always exceptions, writing should move from the particular to
the universal rather than the other way around. Overly abstract
summary loses readers. There are writers who can pull off the
use of abstractions, but if you study how they do it you'll see
that they tend to use them sparingly and have set up for them, as
Tim O'Brien does in *The Things They Carried*, familiarizing us
with all the actual *physical* items that weigh down the soldiers
in one platoon, before briefly moving into the more abstract
things they carry, such as fear.

Study your own work to see if you can locate abstractions. If you can, try to determine if the abstractions deepen readers' understanding of the situation you're describing or if the abstraction will make them turn away. Are you using big ideas such as love, patriotism, sacrifice as abstractions instead of demonstrating them in the particular, with the kind of detail that draws a reader in?

THE SIN OF BEING OBVIOUS— TIRED OBSERVATIONS

When you include reflective summary you want to be sure it is fresh and insightful. It isn't enough to serve up platitudes or familiar commentary.

Brad Newsham is a San Francisco cab driver who traveled to India, Africa, Egypt, and Latin America in search of the perfect stranger to invite back to the States on a visit he'd finance. He is a very appealing narrator and he often does a fine job observing the world around him. Where he loses credence is in his occasional overly familiar reflection:

> India put us into the present moment in a way we'd not experienced before, never giving us a clue about what to expect next, while confronting us daily, almost hourly, with novel or horrifying or heart-wrenching situations, whose resolutions required that we instantly reinvent ourselves, find some new non-Western way of thinking. We finally left, shaking our heads and thinking, there can be no place as mind-scrambling, as tragic, as magic as India.

This is the kind of observation that makes me question the narrator—is there really no other place as mind-scrambling as India? Or has Newsham just not been to a more mind-scrambling place? Compare Newsham and Annie Dillard's reflections on being in the present.

Have any tired observations slipped into your work? Do you find lines such as "He loved her *with all his heart*" or "There is no place like home"? Give your work a read-through and red-line phrases and sentences that have that ring of familiarity to them. Then find a fresh way to get your point across. Push yourself. Do you really agree with a familiar line such as "there is no place like home"? Why is there no place like home? What do *you* think about home?

THE SIN OF PONDEROUSNESS AND PRETENTIOUSNESS

Years ago I read a memoir in which the narrator asserts, "A woman's body remembers." It struck me as the kind of generalized statement that makes oversized, mystical claims. It became a family joke. If I said I craved fish for dinner, my husband would say, "A woman's body remembers." Reflection makes writers vulnerable. You don't want to be in the position of having someone make a joke about your statements. Look over your reflections to make sure they don't come across as grandiose or pedantic. If you find yourself making the kind of comments that set your narrator up as superhumanly wise or benevolent, check the pretentiousness-o-meter. Then scale those observations and judgments back down to size. Rather than a line such as "women hold the mystery of life in their blood," which also fits in the tired observation category, you might want to consider what you, or your narrator or character, *really* think about women and blood. If you sit long enough with each statement that you've noted as pretentious, you'll probably come up with something original and honest, if more modest.

Summary 💬
Exercises

a.) Write a paragraph of summary about a childhood outing in which you use vivid sensory detail.

b.) Write a page of summary that condenses thirty years in the history of a family. Make it interesting!

c.) Create a character using summary; include interior thoughts, external description, summarized behavior, and narrative commentary.

d.) Write a paragraph of summary in the voice of a reflective narrator who just read an old love letter.

e.) Select a published scene that contains interspersed summary. Remove all summary embedded in the scene and read what remains. What has been lost? Has anything been gained?

f.) Write two paragraphs of summary with an eye to narrative layering—one paragraph in which the narrator is a child, the second in the voice of the same narrator from an adult perspective. The older, wiser voice should illuminate the younger, more innocent or naïve passage.

g.) Write a few paragraphs of summary that display the use of repeated time.

h.) Write a paragraph of summary in which the narrator establishes a tone of irony. Rewrite the same paragraph shifting the tone to straightforward and pragmatic.

Combining

Scene and Summary

*N*ow that you are familiar with a range of possible uses of showing and telling independently, it's time to discuss how they can work together to create vibrant and essential prose. In this section, I will take a look at the relationship between the two, concentrating on the ways you can use summaries to set up scenes, control pace by mixing scene and summary, and create transitions. I'll also discuss the role they play in beginnings and endings.

Chapter 10

USING SUMMARY TO SET UP SCENE

*W*hy, you might wonder, do scenes need setting up? Why can't they just stand on their own? Often they can, but jumping from scene to scene without transitions and no setup can sometimes feel choppy. Choppiness is fine if you're portraying the disjointed thought patterns of a distraught or mentally ill character, or stacking up scenes like an album of memories. But when you need your story to flow smoothly, or if you want to increase the impact of a scene by preceding it with summary that provides context or increases dramatic tension, setups can be very useful.

BACKGROUND/CONTEXT BEFORE SCENE

A setting-up summary might last for just a few lines, long enough to introduce the context of a scene, or it can go on for pages, deeply immersing the reader in the character's or narrator's history, feelings, living or working conditions, and so on. You can summarize before a scene, making the summary clearly establish a situation that existed before (and possibly after) the specific time in which the scene occurs. If, for example, your intention is to show the monotonous and hectic life of a young mother with several diaper-age children before an important event occurs (perhaps one of the children can't be found, or swallows a bottle cap, or a strange and attractive man shows up at her door) you could write something along the lines of:

> Marie could never find Jimmy's pacifier and he wouldn't sleep without it. This always required an all-out search— under the washing machine vibrating with another load of soiled clothing, beneath the kitchen table where the dog lurked, waiting for something to fall from a high chair, under the edge of the kitchen counters, in the prairie of dustballs that she never noticed until searching for the pacifier.

Then the scene:

> Marie was crouched to peer under the playpen, in the midst of searching yet again for the pacifier, trying to ignore Jimmy's shrieks, when the doorbell rang one Friday morning …

By using summary first—including markers for repeated time such as "never" and "always"—to set up the scene, I've established the tedium and hectic, disorganized nature of Marie's life before the action begins. Certainly I could write the scene without the summary, starting with Marie crouched when the doorbell rang. I could start with the doorbell ringing, for that matter, but you wouldn't understand Marie's exasperation and you wouldn't have the expectation that this doorbell ringing might bring a welcome (or further annoying) break from her routine. You wouldn't be as eager to read on.

Of course, using summary to set up scenes is useful for establishing situations other than repeated, tedious events that are about to be disturbed by an outside force. Summary can set up scenes by revealing particulars of character and giving useful personal history. Maxine Hong Kingston, in a chapter from her memoir *The Woman Warrior*, focuses on her own silence and the silence of Chinese kids in American schools when she was a girl. First comes the summary and then a crucial scene follows in which she attacks and torments another Chinese girl who is even more silent than she is, in order to make her speak. This attack would be much harder to understand without the context that the summary provides.

We learn, via the preceding summary, about her embarrassment when her mother insists she ask for "reparation" candy from a pharmacist whose delivery boy mistakenly brought medicine to their house and so, her mother believed, cursed them with ill health. We learn that as a child Kingston believed that Americans find the Chinese language "Ching-Chong ugly." Through this extended summary, we also find out that the Chinese kids who are so silent in their American public schools are loud and rowdy in afternoon Chinese school. It isn't the fact of being Chinese, but the fact of being Chinese in the world of white "ghosts," that makes them so silent, and makes the scene of the attack so painful and powerful. Kingston tells us, in summary, her feelings about this other girl: "I hated the younger sister, the quiet one. I hated her when she was the last chosen for her team and I, the last chosen for my team. I hated her for her China doll haircut. I hated her at music time for the wheeze that came out of her plastic flute ... "

The scene begins:

> One afternoon in the sixth grade year ... I and my little sister and the quiet girl and her big sister stayed late after school for some reason. The cement was cooling and the tetherball poles made shadows across the gravel. The hooks at the rope ends were clinking against the poles.

In the scene, time slows down. Kingston takes enormous care setting up the scene, the mood. She even uses summary within the scene to tell you the cost of staying late—the last time her mother called the police to say she'd been kidnapped. We hear about the sounds of the toilet pipes when they are flushed during school hours—the summarizing within scene here increases the tension.

When the attack begins, it is shocking:

> "You're going to talk," I said, my voice steady and normal, as it is when talking to the familiar, the weak, and the small. "I am going to make you talk, you sissy-girl."
> I thought I could put my thumb on her nose and push it bonelessly in, indent her face. I could poke dimples into her cheeks. I could work her face around like dough ... I reached up and took the fatty part of her cheek, not dough, but meat, between my thumb and finger ...

It's one thing to know that she hates this little girl because she hates the silence in herself. This girl has become representative of everything that makes Kingston feel unlike the non-Chinese children—silence, weakness, inability to play sports, being well-behaved. We get the point as she tells us all of this in summary. But we only understand the depth of her fury, her self-hatred and anger at the world, when we see how she attacks this little girl.

Our response to this extended scene is visceral. We experience Kingston's emotions even as we have our own reactions to the events she dramatizes. The summarized parts that precede it evoke a more cerebral response, in which we are given information that will help us see the larger picture. If Kingston had *only* summarized, had she written merely that "In sixth grade I trapped a very quiet girl in the bathroom and demanded she speak," we would feel none of the depth of her emotion and how far it could drive her. And if she'd only written the scene, we would simply think she hated the other girl and her silence; we wouldn't understand that it was Kingston's own silence and embarrassment that drove her to behave so badly.

When you establish a character's behavior in summary by using general time—habitual, repeated, ordinary (as in Kingston's portrayal of her silence and embarrassment)—and then you break that habit, confront the ordinary in a scene in which the character steps out of her summarized behavior (as in Kingston's attack on the other girl), you have a turning point, a moment of change. The ordinary is set up through the summary and the extraordinary follows in the scene.

This kind of summary as setup is particularly helpful with dramatic scenes that require the reader to understand more about the characters than the scene shows because the scene is focused on the immediate actions and words of the characters.

RAISING DRAMATIC TENSION THROUGH SUMMARY BEFORE SCENE

Writers occasionally set up scenes by using summary that not only offers relevant information but creates expectation for something important that will happen in a scene. In Amitav Ghosh's essay "The Ghosts of Mrs. Gandhi," which describes how he got caught in the midst of attacks on Delhi's Sikh population after Indira Ghandi's assassination, you can clearly see the way the preceding summary raises the tension in the scene that follows. Before a scene, Ghosh, in summary, tells us that 2,500 people died in the riots, mostly Sikh men, and tens of thousands were left homeless. He adds:

> … I grew up believing that mass slaughter of the kind that accompanied the partition of India and Pakistan, in 1947, could never happen again. But that morning, in the city of Delhi, the violence had reached the same level of intensity.

This scene follows:

> As Hari and I stood staring into the smoke-streaked sky,
> Mrs. Sen, Hari's mother, was thinking of matters closer at
> hand ... When she heard what was happening she picked
> up the phone and called Mr. and Mrs. Bawa, the elderly
> Sikh couple next door to let them know they were wel-
> come to come over.

Although they have trouble believing it, the Bawas will have to
seek refuge in the Sen's house as the rioting gangs come to kill
them and burn their house down. Ghosh has set us up for the
frightening scene that follows by letting us in on the scale of
the murders occurring across the city and comparing it to the
murderous Muslim/Hindu riots attending the partition of India
and Pakistan. Without this prelude, readers would have been as
innocent as the elderly, privileged Bawas, unaware of their lives
being threatened until the last minute. We are already afraid for
them before the thugs arrive and so the tension has been ramped
up. Ghosh could have put this summarized information *after* the
scene and the reader would end up equally well informed, but
the scene would have had less impact.

Setting up tension through relevant summary before the
scene can be used in less dramatic scenes, not just life-and-death
situations. Even a quick-paced, lighthearted entertainment such
as Helen Fielding's *Bridget Jones's Diary* uses summary to ratch-
et up the tension before a scene, in this case, the scene in which
Bridget meets Mark Darcy at her parents' friends' New Year's
day party, which she's been dreading. Here Bridget relays all the
fuss being made over her meeting Darcy before the party occurs.
Although there's dialogue, it is summarized. The phrases "every
time my mother's rung up" and "then next time" establish that
this dialogue occurs in repeated time, not a scene:

> Every time my mother's rung up for weeks it's been, "Of
> course you remember the *Darcys*, darling. They came

over when we were living in Buckingham and you and
Mark played in the paddling pool!" or, "Oh! Did I mention Malcolm and Elaine are bringing Mark with them to
Una's New Year's Day Turkey Curry Buffet?" ... Then next
time, as if out of the blue, "Do you remember Mark Darcy,
darling? Malcolm and Elaine's son? He's one of these
super-dooper top-notch lawyers. Divorced. Elaine says
he works all the time and he's terribly lonely. I think he
might be coming to Una's New Year's Day Turkey Curry
Buffet, actually." I don't know why she didn't just come
out with it and say, "Darling, do shag Mark Darcy over
the turkey curry, won't you? He's *very* rich."

By the time we meet Mark Darcy—and watch the awful awk-
wardness that ensues at the curry buffet—we are as primed to
meet him as Bridget is not. Of course, he's the man she falls in
love with by the end of the novel. Since the meeting is essential to
the plot, it occurs in a scene. But the tension (and even suspense)
has already been established by Bridget's exaggerated summarized conversations with her mother preceding the meeting.

To use the technique of setting up a scene by creating suspense or tension through summary in your own work, consider
what background information, details, references to themes,
reflection, and so on might be summarized immediately prior to
a scene. It has to be relevant and *it has to create an expectation in
the reader.* Raising an unanswered question is one way of creating expectation. For instance, if we return to poor Sally who
appears in Section I, breaking her ankle on a children's slide, we
could set up tension for the accident to follow. In Section I, I discussed using a flashback to give background relevant to Sally's
soon-to-happen accident. But you can achieve much the same
deepening while increasing dramatic tension by using summary
before the scene. What you want to emphasize (Sally's uncertain
future as a kindergarten teacher; her bad judgment in other

situations; her history of inappropriate outbursts; or her being accident prone) will determine the nature of the preceding summary. If you want to set up for the events to come and emphasize Sally's questionable judgment, you might precede the accident scene with a summary about Sally's errors on other jobs:

> Last year, as a student teacher, Sally had alienated her supervising teacher by bringing a bat to school. It had gotten into her apartment through an unscreened window and she'd caught it in a laundry basket. She thought it would be educational for the kids to see it. Mrs. Garfield hadn't agreed. Sally wasn't going to make that kind of mistake this year.

Immediately the reader wonders, what mistake will Sally make this year? You've set up an expectation and upped the tension. Whether your scene is going to be about a kindergarten teacher or a soldier on a battlefield, you can increase the tension and make your reader eager to read on by employing setup summary.

WHEN SUMMARY DETRACTS FROM THE FOLLOWING SCENE

If your summary pretells something that the scene will show, it will weaken rather than strengthen the scene. Think of going to a movie with a friend who has already seen it. As soon as you settle in your seats your friend tells you how much he loves the first scene in this movie; before you can stop him he goes on to summarize what's going to happen in that scene. You'd probably want to kill him. Well, if your summary tells what's going to happen in the next scene, you've played the role of the annoying friend. You haven't trusted that your scene is strong enough or that your reader is smart enough to get what happens as the scene unfolds. Make sure your setup

Chapter 11

INSERTING SUMMARY IN THE MIDST OF SCENE

*W*riters add summary to ongoing scenes for several reasons. They might want to include important background (or even future) information that will affect the readers' understanding of the characters or narrator. Or they might want to emphasize transformations in characters by including reflection, or control the pace of the scene.

INSERTING EXPOSITION

Summary is often used in the form of exposition in the midst of scene:

> Jane walked to the crest of the bridge and stopped to look into the water. The river was wide and sluggish here though further north it cut swiftly through narrow gorges. Jane dropped a nickel into the slow brown waters. It disappeared immediately from sight.

The purpose of this insertion can be multiple. The first half of the sentence—*The river was wide and sluggish here*—can be simple scene-setting description. The second half—*though further north it cut swiftly through narrow gorges*—takes us momentarily out of the scene. There may be a symbolic reason for this exposition—perhaps Jane feels sluggish and the description emphasizes her mood and her desire for refreshment symbolized by the rushing waters up north. There can be pacing reasons for the insertion as this description momentarily slows the scene (see chapter 13 on pacing, page 181). Perhaps Jane is from the north or wishes to go there and by making reference to it the narrator is complicating the scene—comparing the present location to another that has meaning to Jane. Whatever the purpose, and we can't know without a longer sample, the expository insertion adds texture without interrupting the scene for long.

INSERTING BACKGROUND SUMMARY TO INFLUENCE THE UNDERSTANDING OF CHARACTERS

In Section I, I showed how Edward P. Jones jumped into the future midscene with the line *"long before I learned to be ashamed of my mother"* in the opening paragraph of his story "The First Day." Not only a shift into the future, it is also a quick summary that shapes the reader's interpretation of the scenes that follow it. There is another brief summary midscene, in which the girl mentions begging to wear some of her mother's perfume, *the last gift from my father before he disappeared.* With those few summarizing words, midscene, we've been given a much fuller sense of this family's situation. The first instance of summary refers to the narrator's future change; the second provides background history that informs our understanding of the protagonist and her mother.

INSERTING SUMMARY TO DEEPEN CHARACTER TRANSFORMATION

In the chapter "On the Rainy River" in Tim O'Brien's *The Things They Carried*, the protagonist/narrator has been drafted to serve in Vietnam; he doesn't want to go—he doesn't believe in the war and he's afraid of dying. He drives north and hides out at a fish camp run by an old man in northern Minnesota. The old man, Elroy, never questions what he's doing there. One day the old man takes him fishing and pilots the boat over the border to the Canadian side—without a word, giving the narrator the chance to escape the draft. This fishing trip is relayed in a scene until the narrator is close enough to jump. O'Brien stops the scene to summarize all the thoughts and images going through the narrator's head, a parade of people from his past calling him back. The narrator realizes he can't face the disapproval of his family and community, he can't risk being called a traitor or coward. He tells us: "I would go to the war. I would kill and maybe die— because I was embarrassed not to." Then O'Brien returns to the scene. "Elroy Berdahl remained quiet. He kept fishing ... "

If O'Brien had written this only as scene, we wouldn't have the benefit of the *process* by which the narrator decided to go to war. We'd have the boat, Elroy crossing the line into Canadian waters, Elroy's near silence, and both of them returning. We'd know that the narrator decided not to go to war but we wouldn't know why. The summary inserted into this scene plays a very important role in revealing character motivation and transformation.

There are those who like to write in the "tough guy" mold in which a character's emotions are never exposed. (Hemingway is often credited with originating this style yet even he, on occasion, summarized characters' emotions within scenes—check out the death scene of Catherine in *A Farewell to Arms*.) This style of minimally displayed emotion relies on external cues—what the narrator observes, for instance—to hint at what characters are feeling without coming right out and saying it. If that's your chosen style—if you are writing hard-boiled detective novels, for instance—then you may not be interested in using summary within scene to reveal character. But for most writers, it is a very useful tool. Of course, you don't want to overdo it so the scene is left behind and the inserted summary completely takes over. I'll repeat: Whenever forward movement is interrupted you pay a price in momentum lost. So you want to add only enough summary within the scene to allow us to understand the emotional base and the emotional shift. By emotional base I mean the feelings with which the protagonist (and possibly others) enter the scene; by emotional shift I'm referring to any inward change that occurs in the protagonist (or others) during the scene. Look for places within the action or dialogue of a scene that make a natural point for insertion of summary.

An example of a good place to insert summary in a scene is a natural pause in action or dialogue, such as when a character says something that the narrator or protagonist needs to reflect on. In *The Great Gatsby,* the narrator, Nick Carraway, is talking for a moment alone with Gatsby at Tom Buchanan's house, just after Daisy, Tom's wife, has made it clear that she's in love with Gatsby in front of her husband. Gatsby says:

> "I can't say anything in his house, old sport."
> "She's got an indiscreet voice," I remarked. "It's full of—"
> I hesitated.
> "Her voice is full of money," he said suddenly.
> That was it. I'd never understood before. It was full of money—that was the inexhaustible charm that rose and fell in it, the jingle of it, the cymbals' song of it ...
> Tom came out of the house wrapping a quart bottle in a towel, followed by Daisy and Jordan ...

Fitzgerald stops the ongoing scene long enough for Nick Carraway to come to a realization that is important to the novel's concern with the behavior of the rich. Fitzgerald has placed this moment of reflective realization in a lull in the action—everyone else has gone into the house to get ready for a car trip into the city. It's a natural spot for an insertion of meaningful summary.

This isn't to say that insertions of summary can only take place during lulls in the action. They can occur (within reason) anywhere that the scene needs clarification or will benefit from our more fully understanding characters' histories, motivations, or emotions. But, if you can find a natural point of entry for your summary, all the better.

To test the effectiveness of the summary you have inserted in a scene, make two versions of a scene, one without the insertions and one with them. Compare the two. Does the one without feel deficient or incomprehensible in any way? Now start adding in the summary, bit by bit, rereading the scene each time after an addition. Does each insertion add anything *essential* to the scene? If not, cut out that insertion. If so, leave it in. Read the new version and reconsider: Is anything else needed? Is there anything else that can go? Your new scene with insertions of summary should be both more streamlined and more powerful than your original version.

Chapter 12

INSERTING SCENE IN THE MIDST OF SUMMARY

Although it is seen much less often than the other way around, occasionally writers use a predominance of summary with only a few insertions of scenes. Tim O'Brien provides many good examples of the uses of summary in the first chapter of *The Things They Carried* and uses scene only at a few important junctures. As described in the excerpt in Section II (page 122), the first chapter of the novel is a running summary of all the things a platoon of soldiers carry in Vietnam, and in that listing, O'Brien makes many references to the death of one soldier, such as, "Until he was shot, Ted Lavender carried ... " Throughout the story we're reminded of Ted Lavender's death, and it is this event, *inserted into summary via a scene*, that removes us from the abstraction of general time, repeated events, the lulling boredom and exhaustion and purposelessness of the relentless "humping" up and down mountains, through jungles.

Lavender's death is central, but we never get to know Lavender beyond mention of his fear, his dope, his need for tranquilizers. Yet his death—when it comes in full, dramatized scene—shocks us with the reality of the threat these men live with. The few scenes in this chapter are related to Lavender's death, which occurs when he goes off to pee while one of the platoon is investigating a Vietcong tunnel. Ironically it is when the soldier comes up from the tunnel safely that Lavender is shot. What does this scene inserted into summary accomplish? It's the center around which the general life of these soldiers, their day-to-day existence, spins. It is the underlying source of all terror. It is the cruel joke, the happenstance—killed while peeing. It is the primal scene, in essence, of the story, the one that must be returned to. It is the moment that causes a transformation in the protagonist, Jimmy Cross; previously distracted by his thoughts of a girl who doesn't love him "back in the world," Cross becomes a hardened soldier.

Fittingly, right after the scene of the death, O'Brien returns to his litany of the things they carried. Yes, Ted's death is terrible, real, but just one of many those who live long enough will witness. It's all part of business as usual, on some level. Back to the hump, back to the weight, all told in summary.

Interestingly, the most abstract "things" the men carry are mentioned after the detailed *scene* of Lavender's death. "They carried the weight of memory ... They carried the land itself ... they carried gravity ... they carried their own lives ... the great American war chest." How does O'Brien get away with loading his men and his story with these big summarized abstractions? The reader has come to trust O'Brien through the specificity of the concrete details he has supplied. The particularized summary and the *focused scene* have set us up for the more abstract picture of these soldiers, and all the soldiers like them, who carried the burdens of the war.

Another example of a story that relies almost entirely on summary with a few brief and highly focused scenes is Donald Hall's "From Willow Temple." The narrator of this story is an old woman who recounts her mother's childhood and her own, summarizing over many years and only offering scenes that show the most important and transformative moments in each of their lives: her mother's beloved cousin's suicide at age fourteen; the narrator, at age ten, overhearing her parents argue over an affair the mother is having with a much younger farmhand; and a moment, a month before her aged mother's death, when the mother confuses the dead cousin with the farmhand. The scenes only occur at moments that rock each of their worlds. The rest is summary, perhaps because the story covers two lifetimes over eighty or so years.

As you can see from these two examples, the inclusion of scene in works that are primarily summary based is far from random. The authors have chosen to stop the ongoing flow of summary to focus in closely, through scene, at particular, well-chosen moments that are of utmost importance to the narrator or protagonist. The scenes inserted into the summary are a way of saying: look closely now, pay attention, this really matters.

One caveat: Both of the stories cited above are prizewinning efforts, but there are very few writers who can carry off the piece that relies on summary to the near exclusion of scene, at least in fiction, and not in a book-length work. Creative nonfiction, with its greater reliance on reflection, may be less scene dependent. Still, a comparison of the *Best American Essays* series over the past fifteen years or so shows an increased preference for works that are less like classic essays and use more of the features of fiction, including a prevalence of scene.

Chapter 13

SCENE, SUMMARY, AND PACE

$\mathscr{P}$ace refers to the balance between fast and slow elements of your story, essay, novel, or memoir. We've all had the experience of reading a book or watching a movie that bogs down, and we've also had the experience of reading or watching something that rushes so fast it leaves us behind. To some degree our idea of a pleasing pace depends on our taste. I don't like movies or books that are all action—chases, crashes, explosions—with little attention to character development. On the other hand, I confess to skimming over the more lengthy philosophical and historical digressions in *War and Peace*. I want a story to move along but not too quickly. You might have other preferences.

Aside from taste, establishing the right pace depends on the demands of the work. A thriller might hit a fast pace and run with it; a horror story might use a lot of pages to quietly build suspense; while a family epic that takes place over generations might unwind more slowly. Nonetheless, when thinking about pace it's important to remember that nearly all narratives (leaving out such experiments as the backward story) require forward motion and change over time, whether that change occurs in the narrator/characters or in the reader's perception of the narrator or characters. All aspects of the piece, whether slow or fast, must in some way contribute to the forward movement of the whole.

While keeping in mind the eventual destination, the object isn't to get there as fast as possible, focusing only on the most important scenes, or we'd end up with stories that were little more than "He met her; they fell in love; they argued; they got divorced" or "There were many battles but eventually the war was won; Lieutenant Smith came home to a hero's welcome but couldn't adjust to postwar life." A good story hits these major plot points but allows us to learn something about the human condition along the way.

Most narratives are a mix of faster and slower sections. When a lot of fast-paced action has occurred, it's only natural to give readers some breathing space with a slower section, be it scene or summary. Remember, a scene doesn't mean speed just because it contains actions, nor does a summary necessarily indicate slowness; scenes can be slow because they are mimicking a deliberate progression of time, and summaries can be rapid because they are compressing time—minutes, days, years. Even when there is a lot of action in a scene, it can be described slowly or quickly, depending on the use of verbs, syntax, etc. (You might want to review the section on Time in Section I in which I compare the Michael Cunningham and Bernard Cooper excerpts [see page 144].) When you've slowed things down with a carefully drawn-out scene or reflective summary, you may want to follow it with more lively material soon thereafter. The idea is to find a rhythm that will keep your reader fully connected to the characters through sufficient development but engaged with the narrative as the action progresses. However, if your story is truly action-based and the action is rising toward a dramatic climax, it's okay to allow fast sections to follow on each other's heels until the climax has been reached.

Pace can be adjusted by various means. If your narrative involves a considerable passage of time (as opposed to one day, as in James Joyce's *Ulysses*), you'll want to decide which spans of time require careful examination in scenes and which spans can be compressed with summary such as "Over the next two years Ralph saw his father only a few times." This moves your narrative forward quickly so you can zero in on the parts that require more attention; in this case, those few meetings with Ralph's father. As discussed in Section I, scenes are necessary when you want to create an emotional connection to characters, dramatize events, show conflict, etc. You will want to slow your pace to spend time setting your scenes with description, dialogue, and internal thoughts. You can slow the pace even further by inserting background summary into an ongoing scene, as described above. But you don't want to bog down your scene with unnecessary conversations or irrelevant background exposition, slowing it down to such a degree that the reader loses sight of what's at stake in the scene. It's a difficult balancing act—keeping one eye on forward motion while spending enough time to make the scene feel real.

Here's an example of when inserting summary into a scene is used deliberately to slow pace as well as contribute to readers' understanding of a character:

In an early scene in my first novel, *Tempting Fate,* twenty-year-old Allie has taken a job as a deckhand on an Alaskan salmon fishing boat. She is supposed to stay awake on watch while her skipper grabs a few hours rest as the nets drift. I knew Allie had to fall asleep—she's already been awake for thirty-two hours, but her falling asleep is also a mark of her carelessness, naiveté, and lack of respect for danger. I didn't want her to conk out immediately. The reader would need to know why she was falling asleep, what she risked, more of who she was, and why she would risk it. Moreover, I wanted to create the conditions in which a sleep-deprived, lost, confused young woman on a commercial fishing boat would be lulled to sleep when her life, her skipper's life, and his fishing license could depend on her not doing so.

The scene is intentionally interrupted with narrative summary to both slow it down and to fill in more of Allie's background. It includes a flashback to her meeting her skipper and taking the job, her feelings about the ocean, even her mother's experience with a drowned man as a child. In the entire foreground scene Allie's only physical action is to put her head down, jerk awake a few times, and finally give in. But the movement of the scene is intended to recreate the in-and-out-of-consciousness experience of someone struggling, not very successfully, to stay awake. Had I merely shown the scene without the summary, it would have been pretty dull, short, and not very informative. Besides slowing the action, my intention was to make you care enough about this girl that you are really afraid for her when she falls asleep on watch.

As you revise your own work, keep asking yourself if your narrative is moving too quickly or too slowly. Where do you get bored reading the draft? Where are there holes? Mark those places and consider them carefully. What can you cut or add to make the draft move forward in a manner that is both smooth and compelling?

FOLLOWING A SCENE WITH REFLECTIVE SUMMARY

Occasionally writers follow a scene with reflection provoked by the scene. I'm not referring to an alternation of scene and summary in which the summary may carry the story further along chronologically. Rather, I'm talking about summary that directly addresses some aspect of the scene preceding it. The important thing with this technique is that the reflection must deepen our understanding of the scene or take us beyond the events of the scene rather than restating what the scene has already shown.

Lauren Slater, in an essay called "Black Swans," gives a scene of meeting with a doctor who prescribes Prozac for her obsessive-compulsive disorder. In the scene she asks him to put away a noisy clock because its sound is distracting; she's covered her ears with her hands. He refuses, saying he won't "collude with her disease." He tells her that she has a crippling disease but, " ... now, for the first time, we have the drugs to combat it."

Slater jumps right from this scene into reflection and analysis:

> My mind, it seems, is my enemy, my illness an absurdity
> that has to be exterminated. I believe this. The treatment
> I'm receiving, with its insistence upon cure—which means
> the abolition of hurt instead of its transformation—helps

> me to believe this. I have, indeed, been invaded by a virus,
> a germ I need to rid myself of.
>> Looking back on it now, I see this belief only added
> to my panic, shrunk my world still smaller.

Slater's reflection suggests that there is a downside to treating her disorder with Prozac that goes beyond physical side effects. She has effectively carried us beyond the scene into new psychological territory. She hasn't advanced her story in a chronological sense—she'll do that in a later scene when she describes her physical reactions to the drug. But she has advanced it by deepening our understanding of what taking Prozac could mean to her philosophically and spiritually.

Creative nonfiction writers use this technique of following up a scene with reflection more often than fiction writers, but there are those fiction writers who take the opportunity to bounce reflection off a scene.

Gloria Naylor, in her novel *The Women of Brewster Place,* describes a scene in which neighborhood busybody Sophie investigates (by going through their trash and spying on their movements) two women that the neighborhood decides are "that way." Naylor provides a humorous scene in which rumor-mongering Sophie intercepts and tries to interrogate Ben, the handyman who has entered the apartment of "The Two" to do some work:

> "What ya see?" She grabbed his arm and whispered wetly in his face.
>> Ben stared at her squinted eyes and drooping lips and shook his head slowly. "Uh, uh, uh, it was terrible."
>> "Yeah?" She moved in a little closer.
>> "Worst busted faucet I seen in my whole life." He shook her hand off his arm and left her standing in the middle of the block.

Sophie then goes on to report to her neighbors that Ben told her it was terrible in there (without mentioning the faucet) and the third-person narrator continues with reflective summary, commenting on the gossiping women (ellipses mine):

> Confronted with the difference that had been thrust into their predictable world, they reached into their imaginations and ... stitched all their fears and lingering childhood nightmares ...

The omniscient narrator comments on the action, analyzing the prejudices of the women who disapprove of "The Two," offering a larger picture than those involved might see on their own.

If you decide that your first-person or third-person narrator should reflect on the events that occur in a scene, you might want to reread chapter 9 on "The Sins of Summary" (see page 155). Your follow-up reflection must not only be fresh in that it doesn't restate what has been well shown in the scene but it also can't be obvious, general, or obscure lest your reader wonder why you bothered with it at all. Consider if you have something important to add that will engage readers and enlarge the scope of the story.

Chapter 15

BALANCING SCENE AND SUMMARY

As a novelist, I've always relied a great deal on scenes, but when I completed a draft of my first memoir I worried that I hadn't written enough scenes and that my use of summary might be flattening my story. I looked to nonfiction writers whose work I admired and considered fully dramatized. I was surprised to see how many of them use a great deal of summary between their scenes. Tobias Wolff is a good example. I had read *This Boy's Life* and *In Pharaoh's Army* some time ago, and I remembered both books as vivid, scene-based works. Both books, it turns out, rely more on summary than on scene. Sue William Silverman's book *Because I Remember Terror, Father, I Remember You* struck me the same way. I thought of it as made up entirely of scene. And certainly, in the early sections, when you are seeing the world through the eyes of a very young child lacking the perspective of time and the ability to interpret events, most *is* written in scene. But as the book goes on and Silverman enters her teen years, summary comes more and more into play. In this case, the shift from dominant scene to more summary came about naturally with the changing age of the narrator. I had mistaken the proportions of scene and summary in these memoirs because both of these authors made their summaries so richly detailed.

Different authors use varying proportions of scene and summary depending on their style, tastes, the prevailing aesthetics of the times in which they write, and the expectations that come with various genres. In earlier eras devoid of electronic entertainment, readers had a lot more patience for drawn-out exposition, description, and informative summary than most current readers do. Not so long ago I rewatched the classic film *Midnight Cowboy* and was surprised to realize that the Jon Voight character doesn't make it to New York for quite a way into the film. The filmmakers had taken their time setting up and developing the protagonist's character and background before he headed to New York and failed miserably at his attempt to be a gigolo. I wonder if a modern audience would have the patience to wait so long before the protagonist gets to New York, encounters Dustin Hoffman's Ratso Rizzo, and the major interaction of the film begins. That movie won three Oscars in its day.

As for the balance of scene and summary according to genre, if you are writing a fast-paced, action-packed political thriller, you probably will want to keep most of your summary limited to just what the reader needs to know about the characters and the background of the political situation so readers can follow the story, with a little summary-as-connective tissue between scenes thrown in. Romance writers tend to focus on scenes because their readers' primary goal is sharing the emotions of the protagonist. Science fiction writers generally include considerable exposition to set up the parameters of the imaginary worlds their characters live in. But they too depend on scene for the important events. If you are writing a literary love story, you may want to spend quite a bit of summary space on the characters' individual backgrounds—families, current or former spouses or lovers, and so on—in order to help your readers understand why they fall for each other and what the obstacles are between them. Even the breezy *Bridget Jones's Diary* relies on quite a bit of summary to fill us in between the scenes. Bridget's accounts of her weight, alcohol "units," cigarettes, and calories are in themselves summary, as are many of her diary notations about her desires, fears, and misadventures that aren't recounted in scenes. Much of that novel is carried by Bridget's witty voice, and narrative voice is often best displayed in summary. Fielding uses a considerable amount of summary in between her scenes, allowing us to enjoy Bridget's reflections and commentary.

If you are particularly interested in portraying the role of the past in a protagonist's present life, as the short story writer Alice Munro is, you will use a greater ratio of summary to scene than, say, a writer such as Raymond Carver, who had a tendency to focus on a character's present situation via a greater proportion of scene. The insertion of history or place description can't be a random choice; it must be integrated into the overall intention for the story. That place or family history might in some way echo the events that occur within the scenes. Think of Nick Carraway's fraudulent family history early in *The Great Gatsby* (see chapter 6, page 97) and how it prefigures Gatsby's self-invented past. History is extremely important to this novel; Fitzgerald even ends the novel with the line, "So we beat on, boats against the current, borne back ceaselessly into the past." Place is equally important—Nick Carraway tells us quite a bit about the Long Island communities of East and West Egg and the "Valley of Ashes" (where poor workers trundle about in dust) that we travel through between the Eggs and New York City. Yet my copy of the novel is only 121 pages long! Fitzgerald manages to balance these summaries with the absolutely essential scenes of reuniting with the Buchanans, traveling with the bully Tom Buchanan to meet his mistress, meeting Gatsby, conspiring in Gatsby and Daisy's secret get-together, the rising tension between Gatsby and Tom, and so on. Fitzgerald is able to fit that much history, description, and scene in such a short book because of his economy in making every piece contribute to the whole novel. No history is irrelevant; no description of Gatsby's mansion or the "Valley of Ashes" is wasted—they complement each other and the scenes in bringing us to realize, as Nick does by the end, that the enormously wealthy, callous Daisy and Tom Buchanan are worth far less than the self-made, idealistic pretender Gatsby.

How then do you find the right mixture of scene and summary in your own writing? If you are not working in the genres mentioned above (romance, science-fiction, thriller) with their specific demands, and you aren't choosing to rely mostly on summary for specific stylistic reasons as Tim O'Brien does in *The Things They Carried,* or predominantly on scene as Carver did, like most of us you'll want to find an alternation between scene and summary, showing and telling, somewhere on the spectrum of predominance.

Tobias Wolff uses this alternation beautifully in *This Boy's Life.* Wolff starts the book with a brief, vividly rendered scene. He and his mother are driving west to find their fortune in uranium mining and they're crossing a mountain pass when a truck loses its brakes and hurtles down the mountain, crashing below. His mother puts his arm around him. Ten-year-old Toby realizes that this would be the perfect time to ask for souvenirs.

The scene of the terrible crash sets up the mood of danger and precariousness that will be borne out in the rest of the memoir. Even more striking, though, is our response to young Toby. What an operator! This kid will use any situation to his advantage, and the adult Tobias Wolff is on to him. Wolff wants us to be on to him too, right from the start.

This short scene is followed by a very long summary that fills in background information. (I included an excerpt from it in chapter 8 (on page 143).) In this summary we learn that Toby's mother is impulsive enough to give her car away to a stranger, even if it is a lousy car. We learn some of the mother's background—her life in California as the daughter of a millionaire before the stock market crash, her dream of a past in which she and her mother played at being sisters. Wolff doesn't comment further, but we learn that his mother won't be much of a mother either. She had early days of glory and they were going to retrieve them. The child believes in her dreams and loves her entirely.

If Wolff had started off with all that background about traveling the West with his mother, I would not have been half as interested as I was after that quick glimpse, that shocking event in the scene that opens the book. I'm hooked, and now I can step back to get the context. On the other hand, without the context provided by the summary, with just the scenes, I wouldn't have as full a sense of these characters, their hopes and expectations, their poverty, and the doubtfulness that their hopes will be fulfilled. Both the scene and summary are essential to Wolff's purpose in this book.

Which brings us back to intention. You can't know how much scene, how much summary to use if you aren't clear on what you wish to accomplish in the overall work. Your proportions of scene and summary depend on your being aware of what's at stake in your piece and what you wish to emphasize. That may sound frustratingly vague. It is. There just isn't a formula for how much to show and how much to tell. You have to take into consideration whether you want to engage the emotions or the intellect of your reader at various points in the piece. You probably won't be fully aware of all this in a first draft, but when you go back to revise, ask yourself the following questions, keeping in mind your intention:

- Do my scenes move the plot forward?

- Do they reveal character?

- Do they engage the reader emotionally?

- Do they drag on and show unnecessary details, pointless dialogue, etc?

- Should they be started sooner or later?

- Do my summaries add information to the narrative that is essential to the story? Do they help set up or connect various scenes?

- Have I summarized anything (significant events, moments of change, etc.) that needs to be in a scene?

- Are there places that drag or rush by too fast? Why?

- Does the summary go on so long that the emotional connection is lost? Do the scenes pile up, requiring a breather via summary?

- Does the shift from scene to summary feel smooth?

Chapter 16

TRANSITIONS

*F*ollowing up on that last question in the prior chapter, let's take a look at some ways to shift between scenes and summaries, from scenes to other scenes, and from summaries to other summaries. There are two main reasons for providing transitions in moving from one narrative unit to another. The first is that you don't want to lose readers by confusing them about where and when things are happening. The second reason is that you don't want your work to feel herky-jerky and discombobulated. Your readers should be drawn into your story and stay there, pulled along naturally until the end. If there are a lot of bumps in the road they may be jolted out of the vibrant narrative world that you've worked so hard to craft.

CINEMATIC JUMP CUTS

Sometimes a transition can be as simple as a white space break on the page, indicating a shift in time and place or narrative mode (scene or summary), or even a chapter break. As veteran movie watchers we're accustomed to the cinematic jump cut that juxtaposes one scene against another, and we can follow that sort of leap in our reading in a way that earlier generations of readers couldn't. A scene ends and the writer provides a space break before another scene or a summary begins. One warning with this method: If your scenes and summaries tend to be quite short you'll end up with so many space breaks that your pages will look more like a list than narrative prose, and your novel or memoir may appear to be built on vignettes. There are good novels built on vignettes, such as *Mrs. Bridge* and *Mr. Bridge* by Evan S. Connell. But if that's not your intention, and your scenes and summaries are very short, you may want to come up with other forms of transition besides space breaks.

CHRONOLOGY

Another simple way to keep your readers clear on what's going on in your work is to generally maintain straightforward chronology (the story moving ever forward in time) with, if warranted, clearly indicated flashbacks. In this case, each time you come out of a summary you'd use some kind of indicator of time, such as "*The following Saturday* Melanie found herself *on I-91, stuck in traffic,* when her phone buzzed. It was Bill." The italics here indicate a specific time and place, beginning a scene. A return to summary from the scene could be indicated by a connecting phrase such as "Melanie wondered about Bill's tone for the rest of the day." There's a logical as well as a chronological link between the scene in the car and the summary of Melanie thinking about Bill. The phone call comes first, followed by her thoughts about the call. Both are linked by Bill.

If you are writing chronologically, this can work for you. However, there are many writers who don't care to maintain a straightforward chronology and many good books that don't use one. Well-known practitioners of nonlinear narrative and their nonlinear works include Nobel Prize winner Gabriel García Márquez, *One Hundred Years of Solitude*; Joseph Heller, *Catch-22*; Lorrie Moore, *Anagrams*; Louise Erdrich, *Love Medicine*; and many others. These writers use other organizing principles to arrange their narratives—Erdrich's *Love Medicine*, for instance, about Native Americans, has been called "circular" in structure rather than linear. Nonetheless, she helps us keep time straight by providing dates at the headings of each chapter. And within chapters, her scenes and summaries often move chronologically. Creative nonfiction probably uses nonlinear narratives more often than fiction does, relying on thematic or imagistic organizing principles.

ASSOCIATIVE LINKS

A good method for moving from scene to summary or scene to scene is to use associative links: words, images, or other sensory details that can carry across different locations, time changes, or narrative modes. For example, Pulitzer Prize winner Jhumpa Lahiri, in a story called "Unaccustomed Earth," manages to move from scene to summary within a single paragraph. Ruma, the protagonist, is finishing up a phone conversation with her husband Adam:

> "I need to get going," Adam said. "I miss you guys."
> "We miss you too," she said.
> She hung up the phone, putting it beside the framed photograph on the bedside table of Ruma and Adam on their wedding day, slicing into the tiered white cake. She could not explain what had happened to her marriage after her mother's death. For the first time since they'd met, at a dinner party in Boston when she was a law student and he was getting his MBA, she felt a wall between them simply because he had not experienced what she had ...

Lahiri uses the wedding photo of Ruma and Adam on the bedside table as a device to shift from Ruma hanging up the phone (next to the picture, which catches her eye) to her ruminating on the state of her marriage. It's a clever way of moving us via an image that carries psychological weight, right out of the scene and into summary. The shift has been accomplished smoothly. Lahiri continues summarizing her feelings about her mother's death, her mother's earlier attempt to talk her out of marrying Adam, and her good relationship with her mother following the birth of her son. Before moving into the next scene Lahiri leaves a white space on the page, signaling not only that she is shifting to another scene but that she is changing to a different point-of-view character.

In this case an image, the photo, was used to carry us from scene into summary. You can use images, sounds, repeated words, characters, tastes, and smells to assist you in linking your scenes and summaries associatively.

JUXTAPOSITIONS

You may want to set one scene or summary against another, creating a transition through juxtaposition of the two for ironic or emotional effect. For example, in my second novel, *The Price of Land in Shelby,* I end one scene with a character, a young woman, returning home from court after finalizing her divorce from an abusive husband. She stops along the way to cool off by wading in a river. She remembers swimming her horse across this river as a young girl—an achievement in fast running water; she savors her new freedom and the belief that she won't be dragged down by her ex anymore. There's a space break and the next scene is located at a small-town Fourth of July celebration with her children and a man with whom she's reluctantly started becoming involved. In that scene her new normalcy is destroyed when her ex appears and humiliates and threatens the boyfriend. The juxtaposition here—setting up hope, carrying the hope into the new scene, then dashing it—forms the transition. There's situational irony here, of course, but my intention was to make you feel her discouragement all the more via the juxtaposition.

Consider ways you might juxtapose various scenes and summaries and what effect might result. If you have one scene end, for example, with a character in danger, you might want to juxtapose it against a summary or a scene with another character so the tension increases before you return to the character in danger. In this case juxtaposition builds suspense. There isn't an actual transition creating a smooth run into the next section—rather the abruptness of the shift, in this case, serves your purpose by heightening your reader's concern for the character. The transition exists in your mind—in your deliberate manipulation of juxtaposition—but not in the mind of the reader. This can be very effective if not overdone. You don't want to set up too many cliff hangers or the device will become obvious and tiresome.

Chapter 17

BEGINNINGS AND ENDINGS

BEGINNINGS

I like to distinguish between *beginnings* in the sense of the first pages of finished pieces of writing and *beginning,* as in whatever allows you put pen to paper or fingers to keyboard and start exploring your story. Initially, when you're just starting on a draft, you might be wondering, how in the world can I find a way into this vague, amorphous cloud of a novel, story, essay? How can I allow myself enough leeway (and tamp down my self-doubt long enough) to find my story? Sometimes you just need to prime the pump by pumping out the rusty water before the clear water runs smooth. Therefore, any way in is a good way in. You can't let yourself get stuck in rewrite perfectionism before you find your subject and your story. Just start at a place, a moment, a scene, or a voice that excites you. You'll find your way from there.

Once you have a completed draft, and you're ready to *shape* a beginning in the sense of the final version of the first pages, you'll want to create a beginning that sets up the story to come, creating reader interest and introducing characters, themes, and conflicts that compel us to read on. Until you have a fairly solid idea of what's at stake in your piece and what the themes will be, it's very difficult to craft the perfect beginning. When readers approach a story, they consciously or unconsciously are trying to figure out what world they've entered, what and who matters, why they matter, and who is guiding them through this tale. You won't be able to help them figure this out until you've answered these questions for yourself. Moreover, you might not know what particular references, foreshadowing, or actions will reverberate with the rest of the book until you have your plot worked out and you have made it to the end. That's all right. Many writers don't get their beginnings until they've finished their draft.

Let's look for a moment at the process of Leo Tolstoy, surely one of the giants of world literature. Tolstoy went through major reconfiguring of the beginning, characters, conflicts, and themes as he worked on his novel *Anna Karenina*. According to Tolstoy's translator, David Magarshack, Tolstoy was inspired to write this book by a line from an unfinished Pushkin story: "The guests arrived at the country house." He was working on a novel about Peter the Great at the time. He dropped it to follow his new interest. Magarshack says that the first drafts of *Anna Karenina* begin with the country house party scenes, which ended up in chapters 7 and 8 of the finished novel. (Even Tolstoy's beginning-as-a-way-in differed from his final beginning.) In his first version, Anna was a crude, hypocritical beauty and her husband, portrayed in the final draft as cold and rigid, was the sympathetic character. Vronsky, Anna's lover, was a noble artistic fellow instead of the dilettante he ends up being. Character as well as structure evolved. Tolstoy started with a vision of a woman who flaunts rules but he ended up wanting pity for her. The novel became a condemnation of the society that condemned her.

But where does the finished book begin? Not with Anna, her husband, or her lover, but, after a famous line of general summary and some specific summary, with Anna's brother, Oblonsky, who is in the doghouse:

All happy families are like one another, each unhappy family is unhappy in its own way.

Everything was in confusion in the Oblonsky household. The wife had found out that the husband had had an affair with their French governess and had told him that she could not go on living in the same house with him.

After a few more lines describing the chaos at their house, a scene begins:

On the third morning after the quarrel Prince Stepan Arkadyevich Oblonsky (Stiva as he was called by his society friends) woke up at his usual time, that is at eight o'clock, not in his wife's bedroom but on the morocco leather sofa in his study. He turned his plump, well-cared-for body on the well-sprung sofa ...

Stiva goes on to have an amusing reverie about last night's pleasures, eventually remembering that he's in trouble with his wife, who, after all, is old and worn out (he thinks) and should expect his infidelities. Oblonsky is not an important character in the novel, so why does Tolstoy begin with him?

This beginning accomplishes two things. For one, it provides, on the plot level, a reason to get Anna away from home. She comes to her brother's house to help soothe his wife, distraught over her husband's adultery, and it is while she's staying at Oblonsky's house that she first meets her lover-to-be, Vronsky. On the deeper and more interesting level, the beginning provides a playful, nearly lighthearted contrast (everyone forgives Oblansky his "peccadilloes") to what will happen when Anna falls in love and has an affair. She will be ostracized from society, although her lover can resume his position. She will lose her child. And she will eventually be driven to despair and suicide because of the social consequences of her infidelity. So, we begin with a lighthearted look at the response to a man's misbehavior, setting up the contrast to what will unfold for Anna. Tolstoy couldn't have known he wanted this beginning until he revised his image of Anna and knew that he wanted pity for her. He couldn't get his beginning, most likely, until he got his ending.

Would it have mattered if Tolstoy started in a scene, beginning with Oblonsky waking up, leaving out the paragraphs of omniscient narration about happy families and the chaos in the house? The world might have lost one of its great maxims, but the setup for what's to come later in the novel would still be there. It would be possible to show the chaos in the house soon enough. Well, before I get taken to task for having the temerity to rewrite Tolstoy, let me just say that Tolstoy's slide from summary into scene works wonderfully just as he wrote it. All I want to point out is that the general *purpose* assigned to the beginning pages would be satisfied either way, by showing or telling.

You too can effectively start your piece with a scene or summary, as long as they each meet the general demands of beginnings and the specific demands of your tale. By general demands I mean that they give us an opportunity to be drawn into the world of your story (through well-evoked setting, situation, or character) and give us a reason to keep reading (character, voice, conflict, suspense, etc.). By specific demands of your tale I'm referring to your intention for the piece and what it needs to get it going. In other words, if you're writing a realistic crime drama you might want to start with the crime itself, in scene, or the discovery of it, in scene, before you duck away to introduce us via summary to the detectives who will pursue the case, friends or family members of the victim, and even the victim's background history. By starting with a vivid scene, you've hooked us into wanting an answer for the questions *who did this?* and *why?* These questions will draw your reader on.

If your intention, however, is to create an alternate reality, as in Philip Pullman's fantasy classic *The Amber Spyglass,* you could start with scene but you might very well want to spend some time creating the world in which your story will take place before characters and situations are introduced, through the use of summary. Here is how Pullman begins, establishing a feeling of solid reality in summary before the unreal comes into play, thus allowing us to slide into the fantastic before we know it:

> In a valley shaded with rhododendrons, close to the snow line, where a stream milky with melt water splashed and where doves and linnets flew among the immense pines, lay a cave, half-hidden by the crag above and the stiff heavy leaves that clustered below ...

After three more paragraphs of description, things start to get strange:

> The cave lay some way above the path. Many years before a holy man had lived there, meditating and fasting and praying, and the place was venerated for the sake of his memory. It was thirty feet or so deep, with a dry floor: an ideal den for a bear or a wolf, but the only creatures living in it for years had been birds and bats.
>
> But the form that was crouching inside the entrance, his black eyes watching this way and that, his sharp ears pricked, was neither bird nor bat. The sunlight lay heavy and rich on his lustrous golden fur, and his monkey hands turned a pine cone this way and that, snapping off the scales with sharp fingers and scratching out the sweet nuts.
>
> Behind him, just beyond the point where the sunlight reached, Mrs. Coulter was heating some water in a small pan over a naptha stove. Her daemon uttered a warning murmur and Mrs. Coulter looked up.

Okay, we've shifted from summary to scene and now we have a strange lady who possesses a monkeylike daemon who warns her of a young girl coming down the path, our soon-to-be protagonist Lyra. The mention of the daemon is a bit shocking; imagine how much more shocking and difficult to accept it may have been if Pullman had started in scene, with Mrs. Coulter being warned by her daemon. You might feel a bit at sea before some summary description comes along to ground you in this very different world where humans possess daemons in animal form.

This is all to say that there are simply no rules about beginning novels with scene or summary in the abstract. Here are some beginnings by well-known writers; some are scene, others summary:

> Renowned curator Jacques Sauniere staggered through the vaulted archway of the museum's Grand Gallery.
> —Dan Brown, *The Da Vinci Code*

> Saturday afternoon she drove to the bakery in the shopping center. After looking through a loose-leaf binder with photographs of cakes taped onto the pages, she ordered chocolate, the child's favorite.
> —Raymond Carver, "A Small, Good Thing"

> I read about it in the paper, in the subway, on my way to work. I read about it, and I couldn't believe it, and then I read it again. I just stared at it, at the newsprint, spelling out his name.
> —James Baldwin, "Sonny's Blues"

> As a boy, I never knew where my mother was from—where she was born, who her parents were. When I asked she'd say, "God made me." When I asked if she was white, she'd say, "I'm light-skinned," and change the subject.
> —James McBride, *The Color of Water*

"You must not tell anyone," my mother said, "what I am about to tell you. In China your father had a sister who killed herself."
—Maxine Hong Kingston, *The Woman Warrior*

Marley was dead: to begin with. There is no doubt whatever about that.
—Charles Dickens, *A Christmas Carol*

Scarlett O'Hara was not beautiful, but men seldom realized it when caught by her charms as the Tarleton twins were.
—Margaret Mitchell, *Gone With the Wind*

As you can see from these examples, both scene and summary can be very effective in getting a story underway. Several of them begin with unanswered questions, presented through showing or telling—why was the curator staggering in *The Da Vinci Code?* Why did the narrator's aunt kill herself in *The Woman Warrior?* Why was James McBride's mother avoiding his questions about her past, and who was she, anyway? What shocked the narrator of "Sonny's Blues" in the newspaper? Who was dead Marley in *A Christmas Carol?* Each of these questions invites the reader to keep going to find an answer. But Raymond Carver's famous story "A Small Good Thing," about a baker who harasses a mother who doesn't pick up a birthday cake (he doesn't know that her son has been hit by a car and is dying in the hospital) starts out in the most prosaic way, with the mother picking out the cake design. A little further down the page the baker is described as being abrupt with the mother and coarse featured; he makes the mother uncomfortable. A tension starts to creep into this quiet description of a mother going about her errands. And *then* her kid is hit by a car. Just as flatly, we are informed about Scarlett O'Hara's charms in *Gone With the Wind* but there's certainly no immediate dramatic "hook" starting this, one of the best-selling books of its time. A paragraph later we learn that Scarlett's demure demeanor doesn't hide her lusty and willful true nature, and the tension between what she's trying to present and who she actually is draws us in. It doesn't take long before we start to hear about the war on the horizon.

Even the most ordinary sounding of these beginnings starts to build some kind of tension fairly early on. All of them, whether they are cast in scene or summary, serve to set up events and themes to come. All of them serve the author's intention for the overall piece. The abrupt and creepy baker becomes contrite and gentle by the end of the Carver story. Scarlett O'Hara's true nature comes to the fore in *Gone With the Wind*. You can supply the match of beginning and book for the ones you are familiar with above.

Once you are sure of your own intention, and you know that you've shaped your beginning to set up what will follow, but you are *not* satisfied with your attempt, try switching scene for summary or vice versa. Sometimes a change in narrative mode will give the needed distance or closeness that your piece requires. On the other hand, the problem may not be that you are using scene instead of summary; you may require a completely different starting point. Perhaps you've begun your piece too early or too late (as Tolstoy did in his early drafts of *Anna Karenina*) in the narrative. Consider beginning at another juncture—try writing a scene or summary that occurs before or after your current beginning. Or, if you are writing fiction, try starting with a different character's point of view. I mention all these possibilities to encourage you to experiment. It may take quite a few tries before you find a beginning that's a keeper.

ENDINGS

Much of what I've said about beginnings stands for endings as well. Wonderful books have ended with scene and equally wonderful books have ended with summary. When figuring out your ending, you have to take into consideration the demands of endings in general—they must leave your reader with a sense of closure, if not complete resolution, and, ideally, they should linger in the reader's mind. But you also must consider the demands of your particular work. Let's assume that you've been successful in your project. You've written vibrant scenes and essential summaries. There is significant change (in character, narrator, or reader's perception) over time by the end of your story, essay, or book. Now you're faced with finding a way out.

Dickens ends *A Tale of Two Cities* with a grand statement: "It is a far, far better thing I do than I have ever done before," says the reformed Sydney Carlton as he dies for his twin on the gallows of the French Revolution. Admittedly, this sentimental ending is more suited to the tastes of the nineteenth than the twenty-first century. But characters can have less grandiose recognitions. Some pieces end with classic epiphanies, in which a narrator or character has a realization that will alter the way we think about them or they think about themselves. Sometimes writers end their work with a powerful image or line of dialogue that crystallizes a theme of the piece. Whatever you choose—scene or summary—as an ending, it must be suited to what's come before in terms of tone and content. For instance, Hemingway ends *The Sun Also Rises* with a highly ironic line of dialogue from Jake Barnes to Lady Brett Ashley, his impossible love object: To her comment that they could have had a damn good time together, he replies, "Yes," I said. "Isn't it pretty to think so?" This disillusioned, cynical ending is particularly well matched to a novel about the jaded "Lost Generation" of post-World War I expatriates.

Here are a few examples of strong, and, in some cases, famous endings:

But I reckon I got to light out for the Territory ahead of the rest, because Aunt Sally she's going to adopt me and sivilize me and I can't stand it. I been there before.

—Mark Twain, *The Adventures of Huckleberry Finn*

The creatures outside looked from pig to man, and from man to pig, and from pig to man again; but already it was impossible to say which was which.

—George Orwell, *Animal Farm*

For now she knew what Shalimar knew: If you surrendered to the air, you could ride it.

—Toni Morrison, *Song of Solomon*

Somebody threw a dead dog after him down the ravine.

—Malcolm Lowry, *Under the Volcano*

And even when the teacher turns me toward the class-rooms and I hear what must be the singing and talking of all the children in the world, I can still hear my mother's footsteps above it all.

—Edward P. Jones, "The First Day"

The Adventures of Huckleberry Finn ends with Huck's reflection about his future. *Animal Farm* ends with a moment of scene that is, in effect, a group epiphany—all the farm animals' efforts to free themselves have been in vain, as the pigs have become their masters just as the humans were. Toni Morrison ends *Song of Solomon* with a character's realization/reflection that echoes back to the first scene of the book in which a man jumps off a building in an attempt to fly. Malcolm Lowry ends *Under the Volcano* with a sad irony pointed up by an action—the dead al-coholic protagonist has become nothing but trash. Edward P. Jones's story ends with a sound that crystallizes the theme—the little girl who will someday "learn to be ashamed of" her mother, hears her mother's receding footsteps as she leaves her at school for the first time.

Reflection, epiphany, pointed action, haunting sensory detail—each of these successfully brings the tale to conclusion. Each contains a resolution. Half are scenes, half summaries. When you are seeking an ending for your work, don't worry about choosing scene or summary. Concentrate on pulling your story to a close in a manner that fits what has come before, something that will reverberate and linger. You don't want to wrap up every detail in a neat bow at the end. That kind of ending gives closure, but it won't stay with a reader. You want an ending that resolves conflicts raised in the book or piece—not necessarily happily, not always as the characters might wish, but in a way that remains with your reader, resurfacing at odd moments—an echoing ending that readers will find themselves revisiting, whether they want to or not.

Just as with beginnings, if you aren't satisfied with your ending, try switching scene for summary and vice versa. Or try ending earlier or later than where you end now. Add a scene or a summary to your current ending to see where it takes you. Or see if there isn't a place further back in the story that provides a better ending. As a writing teacher, I've often found that students have reached their ending before their final paragraphs and all they need to do is cut off the last paragraph or page or two. I once had to lop five pages off a story I wrote when I came to see that I'd already ended it quite a ways back with a line of dialogue. In any case, experiment until you're satisfied.

A FINAL WORD ABOUT MIXING SCENE AND SUMMARY

Although it's important to strike a balance between scene and summary, showing and telling, it's crucial to remember that your narrative and your characters must be primary; technique must be in their service, not the other way around. No one reads a book and says, "Wow, that's a great balance of scene and summary!" The scenes and summary will be unnoticeable *as such* to an avid reader—only you will know how hard you've worked to craft them and stitch them together. Still, when your summaries are essential and your scenes vibrantly evoked, when the ratio of one to the other and the shifts among them are effective, they will carry the compelling tale and memorable characters you've created.

Scene and Summary
Exercises

a.) Use setup summary to raise dramatic tension in a scene about a woman who has lost her car keys in a darkened parking lot on a city street.

b.) Now, insert summary into the scene of this woman in the parking lot to deepen our sense of the character.

c.) Write a page in which summary dominates and scene appears briefly.

d.) Write a page in which scene dominates and summary appears briefly.

e.) Take one of the scenes you've written earlier, from these exercises or your own work, and follow it with reflective summary.

f.) Use an associative link to move from scene to scene; scene to summary; and summary to scene.

Sample Story:
"Russia Is a Fish"
by Laurie Alberts

INTRODUCTION TO "RUSSIA IS A FISH"

I wrote this short story quite a few years ago; it received a Katherine Anne Porter Prize. Eventually it became the starting point for my 2006 memoir *Between Revolutions: An American Romance With Russia*. The story, told by a first-person narrator, is about a young American woman, Kate, who fell in love with a Russian man, Kolya, while on a teaching exchange in the Soviet Union. Kate had to return to the United States, managed to get back to Russia, only to find that much had changed during her absence. On the largest scale, the story explores the role the state played in relationships between Americans and Soviets during the Cold War era, as well as among Russians themselves. But on the smaller level, it's an odd sort of love story.

This story makes an interesting case study in the use of scene and summary because it moves through several time frames both in scene and summary and utilizes time tags to help you keep on track. It attempts to create the illusion of real time in the scenes (both forward moving and flashbacks), employs various forms of summary, including compression of time, reflection—particularly when the narrator is thinking about the meaning of the events as they unfold—and informational summary when providing explanations about the way things worked in Soviet Russia in the last gasp of that empire during the 1980s, a time when Soviets could be punished for even meeting with foreigners, a time of closed borders and economic hardship, as well as an underlying richness of life.

As you read it, you might want to see if you can identify places in which I've:

- Used both concrete and symbolic detail to reveal character, set scene, introduce and advance themes, create conflict

- Shifted tense to indicate changes in time frame

- Used interior thoughts, description, behavior, and dialogue to reveal character

- Employed metaphor or simile

- Inserted summary into scenes

- Layered the narrative (in this case by comparing last year to this year rather than by comparing the point of view of a child to that of an adult)

- Moved from scene to summary and vice versa

It's up to you to decide if I've successfully created a balance between scene and summary. I hope that the process of analyzing the way they function in this story will help you to become more aware of, and more proficient in, the use of scene and summary in your own writing. Good luck on your showing and telling journey.

* "Russia Is a Fish"originally appeared in *Nimrod Awards Issue X, Volume 32, Number 1, Fall/Winter 1988*. It also appeared in Laurie Albert's collection *Goodnight Silky Sullivan*.

Russia Is a Fish

On the Gulf of Finland the water is so warm, so shallow, it seems I could just get out of the boat and walk away. The sun hangs forever in the sky. Later there will be lights on the freighter anchored to our west, and in Leningrad, no longer visible in the distance. Vera and I have taken the rowboat and left Kolya and Alyosha on the island. At first they chased us, splashing and making indignant noises, but we were faster and easily left them behind. I turn to look back at them: Kolya, small, wiry, curly haired, a flush of sunburn where his open shirt left his pale skin exposed this afternoon; Alyosha, bulky and bearish, large hands hanging at his sides. Alyosha was probably thinking of the vodka bottles waiting by the campfire.

As we row, Vera sings in Russian, I in English. I have forgotten the words to my American song but it doesn't matter. To Vera, who speaks no English, it is just melodic noise.

"Smotri," I say, pointing: Look. A few hundred yards away a sailboat glides gracefully in from the Gulf, headed toward the river from which we came earlier in the day.

"Idi syuda!" Come here, we call, but the sailboat takes no notice.

They are afraid of us," I venture.

"Like all men," says Vera, and we both laugh.

Vera's spine, exposed by her bathing suit, makes a line of bumps between the strong muscles of her back. Her sinewy calves flex impressively with each pull on the oars. Why are the oars so heavy? Russian oars, long squared-off blocks of wood, they are much bulkier than they need be. When I offer to take a turn, Vera refuses and I relent; I know she is stronger than I.

In the bathroom of a Leningrad discobar last night, a club with an American gangster theme, replete with mockup of a roadster, taped tommy gun shootout, and strobe lights, Vera told me about her life while I balanced over the toilet in the men's room. The woman's room was occupied and the men's had no lock, so Vera came in to stand guard. Leaning against the door, she said she thought she'd die when her husband left her, she loved him so much. How could he could have left her? Watching her dance with Alyosha, flinging her blond hair over her shoulders, laughing, even I was awed. She is strong boned, bosomy, full of joy. The answer is: because. Now she loves Alyosha, who will not leave his wife and child.

"I would not ask that," Vera said. "It is enough for me when Alyosha and I can be together. Like holiday." She turned to hit the bathroom door in answer to a desperate drinker's complaint. "For me it is not so bad because I am not alone. I have my little daughter."

I think she pities me.

...

Last winter, in the soft light of his bedroom, Kolya lay his head on my breasts. "A child would be very comfortable here," he said. "Our child." I didn't expect such words, didn't trust them. Maybe they were what a Russian man thought he must say when he slept with a woman. What American would say such a thing, and so quickly? Yet Kolya spoke so naturally the idea struck me as a revelation.

"It will not be," I said.

"Why not?"

I didn't have the words in my bad Russian then, not even in English if Kolya could have understood my language. The only English he knew was what he called "Beachspeak"—whiskey, woman, my love—words remembered from his seaman days. "You know ..." I gestured at the softly lit room with its standard Soviet beige print wallpaper, at the enormity of the dark Leningrad night and everything about it that confused and frightened me, like the gaii—the car police—who stopped us at a checkpoint to examine Kolya's papers every time he drove me to his house. I could have just as well been gesturing at my purse on the floor and in it my visa, its expiration date clearly marked, a month away. "Because you live here and I live there," I concluded.

"We will be together. I know. We will live here and there."

"It isn't possible."

"It is. There are such people who live this way. Everything is possible if you want it very much. I want, and it will be. Everything can be arranged." He rubbed his thumb and forefinger together in that universal sign for money. "Ya khochu dolgo," he muttered, opening a bottle of vodka with the back of a knife. "I want time."

I sat up to take my glass. "Kolya, we don't even know each other. I speak Russian so badly, when you were telling jokes and everyone was laughing, I didn't even know if your jokes were funny."

"Of course, funny. I have very gipkii mind."

"Gipkii? What does this word mean?"

"Gipkii, gipkii." Kolya reached for the Russian/English dictionary I'd brought as a gift. Carefully he underlined the word in pencil, with all of its meanings: Flexible. Agile.

Such a shameless declaration made me laugh. "Kolya, you are proud," I said, because I didn't know the word for bragging. "You have a gipkii mind and I have gipkii body." Sitting heels together, I leaned over and touched my forehead to my toes to demonstrate.

Kolya ran a finger down my naked spine, kissed me between the shoulder blades. "You are acrobat?"

"No."

"And I was."

"Show me."

Kolya downed his vodka in a gulp, stood naked and tested his weight on a chair.

"No, please, Kolya, it isn't necessary. Only a joke." I didn't have the idiom to dissuade him—you'll break your neck, I was only kidding, if you kill yourself, who will drive me back to my hotel before they lock the door?

Slowly, breathing deeply, Kolya placed both hands on the chair. He kicked upward and hung, jackknife position, balanced horizontally over his hands. His slender body looked beautiful, every muscle tensed, and a single drop of sweat ran down the side of his face. Slowly, trembling, he raised his legs overhead in a perfect arch. The chair wobbled under his weight. Seconds ticked by. Kolya dropped down lightly, slid beneath the covers with me, and grinned.

"Everything is possible," he said.

...

Vera and I turn the heavy rowboat back toward the island. Kolya and Alyosha are waiting. We have grown bored with our mock escape; we only ran away in order to come back.

"I still love him," I say, although I'm not sure if it was ever true.

"I know," says Vera, "I see it. That dirty dog."

...

This morning, Alyosha, Kolya, and I stood in the sun beneath the window of a cement block hospital, waving and calling to Alyosha's wife, Tanya, while Vera hid around the corner in Kolya's parked car. I felt guilty, looking up at Tanya's wan face. A week ago she'd lost their second child in a miscarriage, and now we were tricking and deserting her: Alyosha, me, Kolya, Alyosha's mistress. Tanya smiled down at us from the fifth floor—visitors were not allowed on maternity wards—and lowered a note in a plastic bag. She was glad, she wrote, that we were going on a fare-well trip, that I would have a chance to see more of their country before I went home. She was sorry that she couldn't come with us and be my guide. The truth was, I preferred Vera to Tanya. Tanya was always nervous and dissatisfied. She wanted to make a good impression; Vera wanted to have a good time.

We filled Tanya's plastic bag with food and gifts: sausage, sweets, cognac I'd bought in the hard currency store—off limits to Russians—and a two-dollar digital watch from the New York streets. Tanya hauled the bag up by a rope, while a young man standing beside us called out, "Masha, Mashinka, Masha!" to his pregnant teenage bride.

We drove north from Leningrad to Zelyonygorsk and be-yond, through little towns and settlements, over dusty roads with glimpses of sea through pines and spruce, past train depots, sunbathers in flip-flop sandals carrying inflatable rafts, town squares with monuments to the brave defenders of the moth-erland, enormous red Lenin posters exhorting productivity, in search of a chicken to skewer over our fire. In the trunk of Kolya's zhiguli we had bread, cheese, dill from his grandmother's gar-den, bottles of vodka and wine, but no chicken.

The first store, a grubby cement bunker with glass doors, was closed for its daily sanitation break. A barrel-shaped Russian woman in a worker's white coat and paper headdress waved us away through the glass. There were no chickens at the roadside food kiosks, just the usual cabbage, onions, and an occasional squash. At each stop Alyosha bought a beer, growing more cheerful as his face grew more flushed.

Kolya and Vera drank kvass, a fermented nonalcoholic brew made from rye bread, ladled out of a metal tub on wagons parked by the road. There were too many gaii north of Leningrad, and the usual three-ruble bribe wouldn't save Kolya's license if they smelled beer on his breath. I wouldn't drink the kvass, because the glass, swished briefly on a little sprayer in between customers, was communal and many of the drinkers lined up behind the kvass wagon had cold sores on their lips. My squeamishness shamed me: proof that I wasn't one with the people.

After two hours of futile driving, I protested. "Why don't we just have bread and cheese? We don't need a chicken." What I really wanted to know was why hadn't we brought one from Leningrad, where the chances of finding one were much better? It was so typical a Russian expedition, planned and yet unplanned.

Kolya studied me sideways from the driver's seat, taking my measure with his cool green eyes. "You do not care about your stomach," he said. "That is not good."

I winced at his judgment. He meant I wasn't a real woman, a Russian woman, who knew the sacred importance of food. I was just a spoiled American who figured if you don't have a chicken to skewer for shashlik, you can always get one tomorrow. I'd missed the point that this was a daily struggle; if one was to ever eat chicken, one had to search tirelessly. Perhaps it was my lack of feminine seriousness that made him turn away from me, caused him to change his mind. I didn't care enough about my stomach and so could never properly care for him.

After a few more stops we parked behind a restaurant cater-
ing to Finnish tour busses. Vodka tourists, the Russians called
them, weekend visitors come to escape the dry laws of their
country and to buy booze sold cheap for hard currency. I'd seen
them often, lurching and belching through tourist hotels, leering drunkenly from bus windows. Alyosha disappeared inside
the restaurant kitchen with my three-dollar bottle of Cinzano
and a couple of packs of American cigarettes—treats from the
dollar store—and returned triumphant, dangling a stringy fowl
with its head still on, clawed feet stiff as talons.

Kolya was happy now. "Do you have such excellent chickens
in America?" he joked, eyeing the skinny bird.

"Of course not," Alyosha answered with the intonation of
a properly trained Young Pioneer. "Everyone knows—Soviet
chickens are best chickens in world!"

They broke up laughing. Alyosha popped a Temptations tape
into the enormous box cassette player between his legs, cuddled
up against Vera in the back seat, and we headed north. Eventually, the two-lane blacktop gave way to a bumpy dirt road and
Kolya, feeling safe enough, opened his first beer.

"What does that sign say?" I asked Alyosha in English, nodding toward a large orange placard covered in black Cyrillic
lettering too dense for me to read as we rushed past.

"Restricted area. No foreigners allowed."

"Are you kidding?" I was already breaking the law by going
beyond the legal thirty kilometers outside of Leningrad, the city
to which I was registered. I'd done that several times this sum-
mer, traveling to Alyosha's dacha, but this seemed a little much.
An American caught in a restricted area could be accused of
spying. Foreigners had been imprisoned, even executed for such
an offense; if we were caught, my friends would be in trouble

for bringing me here. Why couldn't we just go camping somewhere else? The risk was part of the pleasure, I supposed, like the Russian passion for adultery—a chance to exert a sneaky independence, a sneer in the face of so much control.

"Don't worry about it," Alyosha said. "You always worry. Remember last year, how you were always afraid?"

It was true. Last year I was terrified that I might break some rule I didn't even know of. I felt guilty all the time. Alyosha used to make fun of me. Walking along the stone embankment of the Neva, past battleships anchored for the Anniversary of the Great October Socialist Revolution, he said, "See that one there, Katie? It has a bomb with your name on it, a bomb just for you."

It wasn't funny but strange: red pennants flapping against the dark grey sky, flames shooting up out of the rostral columns on Vasilevsky Island, a parade of children bearing placards, tanks blocking the streets, and everywhere the enormous airbrushed faces of the Politburo.

And if my fears were so foolish, why did Kolya insist I call only from payphones and meet him on corners, never in front of my hotel? Why did I have to smuggle my key out of the hotel instead of handing it in to the floor lady as I was supposed to, so that they wouldn't know I'd spent the night away from my room?

"I want to see you again and if you don't take the key I cannot," Kolya had said, rising up from the covers to dress and drive me back to the hotel.

"Why not?"

"It is just something I know."

"But then, how is it possible that everything can be arranged for us to be together?"

"We need time to make arrangements. We don't need problems now. There will be enough problems when the time comes."

I believed in Kolya, I put my faith in him. He was cautious, not afraid—the only untamed Russian, a man who could do whatever he wanted. He convinced me of his courage from the beginning—the afternoon, last fall, when he came to find me at the school where I was teaching, appearing on a bench in the dim entry, seated between overcoated babushki and pensioners waiting to pick up their grandchildren.

"You didn't call me," Kolya said, "so, I came."

Why would I have called him? We'd met only once. I didn't need any problems.

Kolya took my elbow and led me past the frightened anger of Galya, my "official friend" at the school, who'd inadvertently allowed us to come together at a sanctioned party at Alyosha's house. Kolya was Alyosha's friend, the unexpected guest.

Outside, in the Leningrad autumn drizzle, two soldiers walked down the sidewalk, a pail of red paint suspended between them from a broom handle. I imagined the pail tipping, the paint spreading over the sidewalk, a crimson pool marking our passage. Nothing happened. One of the soldiers threw a cigarette butt onto the wet sidewalk. Kolya unlocked the door to his car and I got in. "This is crazy," I said in my stilted Russian. "I can't even speak."

"No problem. I will be your teacher."

Out of the corner of my eye I saw Kolya's square red hands on the leather-wrapped steering wheel, and dangling from the ignition a keychain with tacky plastic American dollars. I could smell his cologne, sense the shape of his shoulder beside mine, the hard angle of his cheek. Who was he? What did he want? Maybe this was all some kind of set-up?

"Where are we going?" I asked.

"Straight ahead."

Sample Story: "Russia Is a Fish"

Kolya pulled out into the afternoon traffic: little zhigulis and moskvitches, olive drab army trucks and produce vans. Through the window grim shoppers moved past stores filled with pyramids of mackerel cans, piles of cabbage, political texts. Despite the dreariness, I envied them. Everywhere in Russia, people were touching: roughly, pushing against each other in the peak hour throngs; gently, lovers leaning into one another as the metro trains came to a stop; companionably as girlfriends, grandmothers, couples, and even soldiers walked with locked arms down the chilly streets. Behind their blank, composed public faces, I could feel the mysterious warmth of flesh radiating like well-banked stoves.

I had begun to think that I was the only lonely person in Russia. In New York—where the *Times* reported that every Saturday night, beautiful, talented women went home with a pint of Häagen-Dasz to watch *The Love Boat* on TV—loneliness seemed normal; here it was an aberration.

Driving with Kolya that day, I had the sense that if I looked hard enough through the car window, I would see myself moving among the shoppers, following my usual lone route to my second-rate hotel. I'd eat supper in a dining room where groups of Soviet tourists from distant republics—Uzbeks, Georgians, Tazhiks—silently hunched over their bowls of soup in shifts. I pictured myself wandering at the edge of the crowds, safe and correct, while another incarnation sat beside Kolya, about to be swept away. When we turned a corner, the first Kate kept walking. Our paths had already diverged.

He drove me to a little settlement of dirt roads, hand-built wooden houses with decorative windows, fir trees, and a whiff of salt from the Baltic. There were no soldiers here, no police, just an old babushka waddling down the road in rubber boots.

It reminded me of Maine: the sailboat under a tarp in the yard, a junked car, fruit trees, an outhouse. Inside Kolya's quarters (behind a locked door I could hear his parents shuffling around, two sets of thumping feet I never met) there were shelves of Pushkin and Turgenev, Balzac and Hemingway in translation, carvings and curios from Egypt, Cuba, Brazil. Wind rattled the window panes. A radiator hissed. Lifting my coat from my shoulders, Kolya said, "This will be your home."

...

Rowing to the island today I put on Vera's yellow-visored cap, something that might have advertised John Deere tractors, and leaned back against the thwarts of the boat. I pulled my black cotton skirt over my bikini bottom to further tan my legs.

"The hat suits her," Kolya said. "The color."

I pulled the visor lower and peered out at him warily.

"She looks like Mona Lisa."

We rowed past kids on a dock who shouted at us. A brown horse watched from behind a fence. In the channel, the water sparkled mercilessly. A speedboat zipped past. We slid by fishing boats and racks of nets. Alyosha rowed, sweating and squinting in the brightness. With every stroke he revealed a small rip on the inseam of his jeans, and the swatch of hair that he'd carefully combed across his premature baldness fell down over one ear. From time to time he looked up at me and winked.

"It is so beautiful here," I murmured. "This is just where I want to be."

"I try," Kolya said.

The words sounded mocking. That was what he used to say when I praised the caviar he brought me, the touch of his hands against my skin. I reached out a toe to tip him backwards into the water but he laughed and leaped overboard, to come up shimmering twenty feet behind us, shaking the drops from his hair.

I wanted to say to Alyosha, row faster, let's leave him behind. I wanted to jump in too, but I knew I wouldn't be able to pull myself aboard and didn't want them to have to haul me in like some lumbering sea creature at home neither in water nor air. Kolya swam easily up to the boat, lifted himself in. Water ran over his smooth white skin, his taut muscles. I raised my camera to frame him in the viewfinder. Kolya ducked his head.

...

Before I left last winter, he gave me his photograph album and told me to take what I liked. These are the photos I chose: Kolya as a child of three or four, wearing an outsized Soviet seaman's cap, in baggy shorts, arm around another, smaller child. Kolya age five, staring intently into the camera with knit brows, behind him a boggy landscape of forest pools and birch, and in his hands a bouquet of wildflowers. Kolya as a young seaman, dreamily gazing over the rail of a ship. He wears a cowboy hat; its strap bent over the jut of his cheekbone, and the coast of Cuba tilts on the horizon. In the last picture, Kolya is a grown man with a hardened jaw and a bandaged hand, raising the sail on his boat.

"In every picture there is water," I said.

Kolya shrugged. "Only on the water do I feel free. No one to tell me what to do."

I closed the crumbling album, handed it back. "I do not know why, but now I am sad."

"Of course," Kolya said. "It is my whole life."

Without me.

There was one photograph I do not have and we were both in it. It was a photo in a stranger's wedding album: Kolya and I at a Leningrad Wedding Palace, standing at the back of a wedding party, caught in the flash when the photographer jumped out to record the moment. Kolya had taken me there as though to preview our future. What would that couple think, years later, poring over their album? They would see us joined, unwittingly, our unknown faces there forever, maybe longer than their marriage lasts. It was the only picture of us together and no one will know what it means.

...

So this is Kolya's Island. A sandy clearing in the midst of marsh weeds and willows. We beach the rowboat and set up our campsite. Kolya erects his Finnish tent. Alyosha gathers downed wood and hacks it into kindling. No, I cannot help cut the onions, that is men's work because it makes the women cry. Vera cuts up our chicken. Rest, they say, you are our guest. When I beg to help, they give me the cucumbers to wash. Standing up to my calves in the warm water, I call out to Kolya.

"What do you think? Do cucumbers sink or float?" I hide the cucumbers behind a log and watch them drift down, narrow green submarines at rest on the sandy bottom. I see myself standing there in my bikini, haloed in sunlight, wanting too much to amuse.

Kolya considers. "If they are good, they sink, bad they float."

In Russian, the word for float, the word for swim, the word for sail are the same.

Alyosha says, "Kate, do you know the anecdote about the deaf babushka and the cucumbers?" He stands there, belly stretching the top of his bathing suit, happy and unselfconscious. "So, two babushki are riding the electric train. One says, ''Oi, there is so little rain this year the cucumbers are only this big.'" Alysoha holds up his palms, two inches apart. "'Don't worry, dear,' the deaf babushka says,' the most important thing is that a man be good.'"

"That is good," Kolya says to Alyosha, nodding in my direction. He means the way I look. The compliment feels like an insult. When I strike out in the water, away from them, Kolya says, "She swims well." Why does he speak of me in the third person? A hundred feet out I stop and tread water.

"Kate," Alyosha calls to me in English. "You must make decision. Which of us do you want?" It is odd how his voice in English always sounds higher, almost priggish, whereas his voice in Russian is guttural, sly.

"Neither," I answer, also in English, looking nervously behind him to where Vera is peeling potatoes, sitting in the rowboat, tapping her feet to the music from the boombox: Linda Ronstadt. Does Kolya know? Does Vera know? The night Tanya went into the hospital I spent in Alyosha's bed. It wasn't what I wanted, merely circumstance—too much wine, a mistake. I didn't want Alyosha, I wanted to be wanted and Kolya had disappeared. Perhaps I wanted vengeance.

"I don't want either of you," I shout back. "Let's see who else shows up."

"Speak our language," Kolya demands. "We speak Russian here."

We gather around a blanket, drinking vodka and waiting for the chicken to cook over the fire. Two small boys appear in our clearing, carrying their shoes. Walking home for dinner through the shallow water, they used our island as a short cut. Vera takes two of our precious oranges and tosses one to each boy. "Opa!" she calls. They both look startled and fumble their catches. I feel diminished by her gesture—Vera who gives without thought.

"That one," Kolya says, nodding toward a curly headed little boy of nine or so with rolled pants. "He reminds me of my Sasha."

Now I feel chastised. Only a monster would want a father to leave his son. But it was Kolya's idea. He said ...

Clutching their oranges, the boys hurry off without a word. Kolya tells a long anecdote in a Russian too rapid and slangy for me to follow. I grow restless, bored. He used to translate everything for me into simpler Russian. He used to say we understood each other perfectly. We had our own language. We were odinakoviye—alike.

Vera watches my face. "Speak more slowly," she admonishes.

Kolya says bitterly, "Kate understands more than she admits. You have to be careful what you say in front of her. It's the same with her camera—you don't know what she'll do with those pictures."

I am shocked by the depth of his suspicion. When did I become such a threat? Last year I was afraid of everything; now Kolya is afraid of me. I rise and wander away from the fire to sit on a rock by the edge of the water. Over the Baltic the sun has begun to set. I commit this scene to a memory already choked with scenes: the lights on the freighter, this slate-colored sea. What will I do with all these pictures, this burdensome album?

Kolya walks up behind me. "When I was little I came here often," he says. He speaks slowly, enunciating every word too well. I want to say, I'm not that stupid, my Russian isn't that bad. He is simplifying his language because he knows why I left the fire, or there is a text beneath his words he wants to be sure I understand. "For me this is home," he adds.

"It's pretty here," I say deadpan.

Kolya sits down on the rock beside me, stares out over the gulf. The beauty of his jagged profile feels like a punch in the chest. He looks like a smaller Neal Cassady, Kerouac's crazy driver in *On the Road*. I'd rather see him ugly now, the shockingly little, wizened Kolya in a synthetic Soviet suit who came to greet me in front of a metro station the first day I returned. We'd driven aimlessly around Leningrad while I, in a fit of nervous sabotage, told him that back in America my sister had just lost her job and my father was going bankrupt.

Kolya tosses a pebble into the water. "Soon this place will not be. They plan to make a new harbor here and fill this coast with sand."

"Kolya!" I flash with sudden anger. "How can you live here? First they took your house, and now this." Kolya's hand-built wooden house is being torn down to make way for high-rises with plumbing and conveniences. It will be bulldozed away in a week or two. His parents have moved to a new apartment, but Kolya, who wasn't legally registered with them, is living out of his car.

"Kate. Katya. It doesn't matter if this place goes. There are many beautiful places. See that island there?" He gestures toward a dark shape across the water. "Someday it will be possible to live there. Perhaps there I will build a house. Come back and I will show you."

"I'll never come back," I say angrily. "You told me to come back, and then you didn't want me.."

Kolya sighs. "Katya, this is a conversation that will not be."

"It will be! Last year you were different. You wanted to make plans."

"Last year was last year. This year is different."

"Explain!"

"Ah, you are American. You want explanations, everything in a little box. We do not need such explanations. Listen, Katya. I do not want you to think I have done badly to you when you go home, so I cannot be alone with you now. You want me to do something I cannot do."

"I don't want you to do anything you don't want to do. And you've already done badly. This was your idea, Kolya. You told me to come back. You said you loved me."

Kolya softly says, "I loved you at the dacha."

"But not now." It was true, he had loved me at Alyosha's dacha two weeks ago, been the old Kolya then—careening through the woods over muddy ruts, happy at the wheel. "Do you have such roads in America?" he'd asked.

"Yes, where my mother lives in Maine, the roads are just as bad."

"Ours are worse!" Kolya had joked, hitting the steering wheel, making fun of the usual Soviet maxim, "Ours are better!"

Alyosha's wife Tanya had passed me blueberries from a pail in the backseat and I offered them to Kolya, who insisted I place them directly against his lips. How happy he'd looked, kissing my fingers, smiling sideways at me. Alyosha's tape deck blasted American tunes: "Been Lonely Soooooooo Long." They thought it amazing when I claimed to be able to tell if a singer was black by the sound of his voice, and not even Alyosha, with his pedagogical institute English, could decipher the words to the songs.

In Alyosha's hand-built sauna, Kolya and I had clung to each other sweatily until Alyosha's mother came in to beat us with birch twigs. Later he led me up to the room that Alyosha's wife had prepared: fresh flowers in a vase, lacy curtains, a beveled glass mirror—like a bridal suite, if not for the single bed. In the morning we lay in the sun beside a lake, awkward again. Kolya took a ring from his pocket. He said that his son had found it and given it to him as a gift. I turned the cheap metal in my hands:

a horseshoe mounted on a circle of tin, a five-and-dime ring, if there were such things in Russia.

"It is strange," Kolya said, "although my hands are not large, they are too big for this ring."

I slid the ring on my own left hand, the American wedding finger. In Russia, wedding rings are worn on the right. The ring was too big for me; it tilted, swung upside down, twirled uselessly. I slid it off and handed it back to Kolya, this good luck symbol, this ring from his son which fit neither of us.

In the face of so much silence, I took an inflatable raft and paddled away through tangled weeds, over water that sparkled like broken glass. Across the lake, swimmers at a public beach shrieked with simple joy, the thrill of cold water. Kolya looked vulnerable, lying curled on a blanket, a small wild animal cringing in open light. I wanted to go back, to put an arm around him and say, never mind, but I couldn't. Everything had led up to this moment and now it was crumbling as Kolya's house would crumble.

He'd left after lunch on a trumped-up excuse. Alyosha and I stood under a tree in the forest, holding berry pails while a warm rain soaked into the moss at our feet.

"You know," Alyosha said, "when I was student, I was given permission to go to England to study on exchange. The day before the trip, they called me in and said don't bother to pack. No explanation. For a long time I was bitter and wanted to leave my country. I got over it."

"But why won't they let you travel? Why are they so afraid you won't come back?"

"Katie," Alyosha shook his head. "We don't ask why anymore. Sometimes it is better not to ask."

At the house, Alyosha carried wood and heated the sauna; I swung in the hammock humming dirges to myself while pregnant Tanya plied me with fat strawberries from the garden. "Speak to Alyosha," she said. "Maybe he knows."

"I don't understand," Alyosha said, "I thought you two were together."

"No."

Alyosha held a hammer, stared at the unfinished walls of the dacha attic while I sat before him on a block of lumber. He'd built this three-story wooden house alone, without power tools, but still hadn't finished this upper floor littered with scraps and nails.

"I don't understand," Alyosha repeated. "Before he got this new job, just a few weeks ago, he was talking about when you'd come back, making plans. He was always singing your praises. He didn't forget you."

"Now he has changed."

"Kate, even I don't know him now. Since he began this new job he is different man. Always busy, always nervous, always taking these strange trips 'on business.' He has problems now. After you left he went from his old job. He had no money, no work for a long time."

"Why did he leave his old job? Was he fired?"

Alyosha waved the question away with his free hand. "Problems."

"Because of me?"

"No. I don't know. Something. Kate, listen, he is crazy! If it were not for all of this now, the dacha, Vera, my child, I would change places with him gladly. I would go with you."

I let Alyosha's comment slide. What was it? A compliment, an admission, a secret desire that had nothing to do with me?

"Kolya doesn't want to leave his country," I said.

"I never thought Kolya cared where he lived."

"That is what he said last year. Now he cares. He says, "You have your problems and we have ours. I am accustomed to our problems."

"He is a fool! He is out of his mind!" Alyosha shook his head, looked around the chaotic room, sighed. "There is so much work to do here." He sat down on the block of wood beside me and put an arm around my shoulder. "Katie, let's have a cigarette."

...

On a rock looking over the Baltic I turn back to Kolya. "You said you wanted us to have a child."

Kolya smiles ruefully. "Let's."

I kick angrily at the water.

"Katya, do you want me to leave my country? Do you want me to leave my son? I have to build him a life here."

"Last year you said we'd live here and there, that he would grow and join us."

Kolya let out breath. "That would have been better."

"You said it was possible."

"Now it is not. Listen, our relations are too complicated. Nothing is possible now."

But why? Because Brezhnev died and there are new laws against the petty, everyday influence dealing that put rubles in Kolya's pocket that would have allowed him to "arrange" for us? Because he lost his job, his house? Did someone put pressure on him, or was he simply unwilling to take the risk? Maybe he lied from the beginning? Or he just didn't care enough?

I want an answer, as though the knowing will relieve me of this loss. I am intent not on having Kolya now, but an explanation. He's right, I am American and I believe in answers. I believe in history. He thinks he can rewrite our past to suit his present—a national trait. I want to beat him about the head with the memories he left me with. What about the candle he made me light at the ikon of Saint Nicholas, patron saint of travelers and seamen, in order to ensure my return? Has he forgotten the smell of incense, the guttering dish of oil, the waving finger of the babushka who reprimanded us, saying it was not permitted, holding hands in church?

Yet there is something suspect in this history, memories I played over and over at home, searching for one more word, one more gesture. I turned my waiting into a cult, a religion, staring at the photographs of Kolya every night, playing the gypsy record he gave me. The memories meant too much—I asked them to bear the weight of my whole life.

At home all spring, waiting to come back, I carried a secret that filled all the spaces. No one knew or could understand my particular drama, not even my closest friends. Walking up Columbus Avenue past the glittering shops, the smug, overdressed couples, it no longer mattered that I was alone. I was special, by virtue of my vigil, my hopes. Kolya's Russianness raised me above the ordinary, made me unique. I didn't have to be especially talented or ambitious. My life was shaped by necessity it had always lacked. Kolya had given it shape.

"Katya, do you want to live here?" Kolya asks quietly.

I look out at the darkening water and think, yes, if it were always like this. But I can't help picturing the city in winter: slushy streets, trolleybuses, burdened babushki toting plastic bags of cabbage and sausage, the omnipresent soldiers and police. "I don't want to become a babushka," I say sheepishly.

Kolya strokes my tanned arm. "Like this is better, true." Then his voice changes, grows suddenly contemptuous. "Here we are not afraid to grow old."

He is selling himself a bill of goods, building a case against me because there is no answer to this puzzle. Neither of us can solve it, neither of us can bend.

"I'd live here for a year or two," I say. "After that, no."

"And I? I am not like you, Katya. If I leave I cannot come back. They will say I have betrayed."

It's true, the risks are all his, and it is terrible for him to have to admit his powerlessness—Kolya who could do anything, Kolya who did a handstand on a chair. Still, I can't stop myself from saying, "But last year you said it was possible." I hear the child's insistent whine in my voice, the stupid repetition, the seven-year-old protesting: but you said. "You said you loved me, Kolya. I never said I loved you."

"Do you?"

I want to say yes. I want to believe it, or want to wield such love as a weapon, as further proof of Kolya's crime, his betrayal. "I cannot love anyone who does not love me," I say stiffly.

"I also cannot. Katya, you too have changed. Last year you were so afraid, and now you are not afraid but you invent problems. You search and search. You are not satisfied with yourself. It would be better for you if you could simply live."

"I was always such a person. I haven't changed."

"I understand you," Kolya said softly, rising. "Because I am the same. Always thinking. If you lived here we wouldn't be together long. We are too much alike."

I listen to him move away without turning my head. Too much alike? Now he damns me for what he used to praise. We are not alike!

"Come join us, Katinka," Vera calls out. "Dinner is ready." She parts the willow trees and appears, blond hair tangled with leaves, large breasts jutting in her overbuilt one-piece bathing suit: a beautiful figurehead riding the prow of a ship. Vera sits down beside me. Her bare toes on the rocks look strong and square.

"Only I understand you," she says, touching my hair.

"At least you still have Alyosha," I respond stupidly, selfish with my loss.

"Phew." Vera laughs. "Who knows? They say, I love you, I love you, but you must never believe. It is how they are. When they say it, they mean it, but they mean only for one day. So you must enjoy that one day."

"For you that's enough?"

Vera's smile is edged with weariness, the lines about her mouth suddenly deep. "What choice is there?" she asks.

We sit by the fire, poking the logs, gnawing chicken on skewers, drinking wine, drinking vodka. The clearing darkens and falls into shadow. When the sun disappears the air turns chill. Now it is August, hinting of the wet, overcast autumn to come—in July the sun never went down at all. Kolya grows oddly attentive, the gracious host, filling my glass, offering morsels. He doesn't have to be afraid anymore—I'm leaving tomorrow.

When all the vodka is gone, Alyosha complains that he is wet and cold. Vera says, "You needs exercise to warm up," and pulls him up from the fire. "Opa," she shouts, running at him across the sandy clearing. She leaps onto his back and they fall. Laughing, they rise, and Vera backs off for another go.

Lurching a bit from the vodka, I get up and trot across the darkened sand to join Alyosha and Vera. I'll leave Kolya to his empty solicitations, I think; I'll show him. Vera and I struggle to hold Alyosha down. Without realizing quite how I got there, I find myself lying with my legs around Alyosha's waist, being dragged through the sand. I giggle hysterically as the sand slides into my clothing, my hair. Only inches away, Vera is whispering to Kolya, who has her pinned. "Stop," she says, "you're hurting me. Please stop."

"Enough?" Kolya whispers. "Enough?"

I can't stop laughing and my arms are still around Alyosha's broad back, but the wave of jealousy is enough to take my breath away. When Alyosha and I rise, the two of them are gone.

Now the game is really over. Alyosha and I sit uneasily by the fire. How silent it is. It wouldn't take much time, the two of them grappling in the bushes. We've all drunk too much.

"Where have they gone?" I ask in English.

"I don't know," Alyosha says. "Why don't you go look for them?"

"I don't want to."

"Katya," he says. His voice sounds pained. "Does it really matter?"

"Vera wouldn't do that to me," I say plaintively.

"Why not? To get back at me. She is not stupid."

The silence vibrates with betrayal. I have betrayed; I have been betrayed. There is Vera and there is Alyosha's wife Tanya. What does my knowing them both mean? I see a quick picture of Vera and me hiding in the kitchen of Alyosha's apartment when his wife's grandfather came to the door to ask how she was doing in the hospital. I conspired. But there is more: Alyosha kissing me on a hot sandy beach. Vera must have known. She is not stupid, nor is Kolya. We have all betrayed.

"I must go find them now," Alyosha says. "Or I will lose my good friend." I do not know which one he means—Vera or Kolya. If he were speaking Russian instead of English, I would know by the noun ending, the built in acknowledgement of gender. It seems ironic that Russian should be more precise.

But then, Kolya appears out of the forest and Vera from the other side of the clearing, where the boat is tied. She is dripping wet, wringing her long hair. I wonder if she had time to circle around the tip of the island, to fake coming from another direction. Does it really matter? Alyosha leaps up joking, too obviously relieved. He doesn't want to know. It is the same as in the forest with our blueberry pails.

"You've been swimming?" Alyosha asks joyously. "Now I want to swim too. Vera, will you join me?"

"But of course," she purrs.

Kolya goes into the tent and I follow. He slides his fingers under the blankets tentatively, searching under my sweater. We can hear Alyosha's and Vera's muffled laughter from the direction of the boat. I turn to Kolya, but when we begin to make love, I say, "With you I cannot."

"What with me?" He hasn't heard. He sounds amused, as though expecting a compliment.

"I cannot." Last year we made love so often we hardly knew when we began and ended. Kolya saying, "This is good, good, good," and me laughing, "Whoever said it wasn't?" Now it feels too much like swimming when tired, trying to keep my head above water. I can't anymore.

I roll away and we lie silently side-by-side in the tent.

"When will you come back?" Kolya asks gently.

"You want me to come back but not for you."

Kolya sighs. "You will come back many times," he says, "but you will never live far from your own country. Here we live well. We are good company, you, me, Alyosha, Vera. You will come back."

"With a husband."

"No problem. Leave him in Moscow and come here." Kolya kisses me with such passion it brings tears to my eyes. "Katya," he says, "I remember everything."

Vera and Alyosha shake the tent violently. "Can we come in?" The four of us lie crushed together, Alyosha against one tent wall, then Vera and me, then Kolya, who is turned away, not touching as much as possible in this crowded two-man tent. I am sure that in the darkness Alyosha and Vera are wrapped in each other's arms. In the breathing silence of the tent, Vera begins to speak, amazingly in English.

"My friend," she says to Alyosha. It is a tiny child's voice, her voice in a foreign language. They are words that come from classrooms so long ago they are distorted by the distance from memory to mouth. "My friend," Vera repeats, "I so happy when I with you."

"AM," Alyosha corrects. "I AM so happy when I AM with you."

"Leave her alone," I protest. "She speaks well."

Kolya lies silently beside me. I feel him listening attentively to the sounds of the words, like a dog.

"Our children are like intelligent dogs," the teachers in the Russian school used to say. "They understand everything but they cannot speak."

And do they obey their masters? I wanted to ask.

"My friend," Vera says. "My dear, dear friend."

This island is another country, and whatever language we speak here is not spoken anywhere else. It is the language of one day only and there are few hours left to this night.

...

Through the long months of winter and spring, I dreamed of a country like this. I dreamed of a sailboat, and white Leningrad nights.

The water glittering and a line of coast black with firs, like in Kolya's picture. We moved lightly over the water, the sail filled with wind. When Kolya released the mainsheet we drifted slowly into a warm, sweet-scented dark. It couldn't have been so dark that time of year.

While we drifted, Kolya laid out pieces of paper, sliced sausage, and bread with a pocket knife. The oily sausage ripped between my teeth. For hours we floated, until the water grew shallow and ahead of us we saw an unfamiliar coast. The keel bumped against the sandy bottom. When we got out we were standing thigh deep in the sea, on the shore of an unknown country. It wasn't my home or Kolya's, but a place where we could live.

...

In the morning Kolya dismantles the tent; Alyosha and I scrub the dishes with grass and sand. We are drinking tea, numb with hangovers and too little sleep, when the uniformed border guard appears in the clearing, a rifle in his arms. My heart simply stops.

Kolya, Vera, and Alyosha exchange glances. "Don't worry," Alyosha whispers to me. "Just don't open your mouth."

I look about wildly. The clues—the Cinzano bottle, the Marlboro packs—were exchanged for the chicken. We are all Soviets here. The guard stops before us. Every aspect of him stands out sharply, surreal in its detail: a belt buckle with the five pointed Soviet star. The creased leather of his belt. His bland, square childish face with its eerie pale eyes—a Slavic clone, like the teenage soldiers in the airports. If he addresses me, my life will be over.

"Spichki?" he says.

Matches. He wants matches. Alyosha offers a light. The guard fumbles for a cigarette, resting his rifle against his hip, lights up, smiles. One of his front teeth is steel; it catches the morning sun. He draws on his cigarette, pleased with himself. Noticing the empty vodka bottle, he taps his throat with two fingers, the sign for drinking. "A good party, eh?" He is just a simple soldier boy, on lonely forest duty.

"Very good," Alyosha says. "Too bad you couldn't join us."

When he is out of sight, Alyosha says, "That reminds me of the anecdote about the border guard."

I can't listen. My heart is still beating too fast, I am sick from the ebb of adrenalin. Across the fire, Kolya gouges at embers with a stick.

Alyosha turns to me. "You can talk now. The guard is gone."

I don't know what to say.

"She didn't understand the joke," Vera explains. "You spoke too fast."

Kolya says quietly, "She understands everything perfectly."

I understand that I will never understand. They live well here, but every moment must be surrounded by a border guard to make it precious. We are alike and not alike. They live under water and I in air. When I look into the water I envy the richness of their world, its density and unaccustomed pressures, yet if I were to stay down there I would drown. And they would suffocate above the water, in all that intoxicating air. Our meeting point is only at the surface and we must all hold our breaths.

...

The four of us sit in the rowboat, piled with dirty pans, empty bottles, and blankets. Now it is Kolya who rows. Again the sun is shining and the sky is a perfect brittle blue. The thwarts of the wooden rowboat are plastered with tiny, glassine husks of winged insects.

"Why so many?" I ask. "Why have they all died?"

Alyosha shrugs away my question. The answer is too trite: The Russian equivalent of June bugs, they spent their one day in some wild carouse.

We row around the island, across the stretch of gulf, to the mouth of the river. It is early still and inside the channels the fishermen are arranging and mending their nets. A few of the small wooden boats are heading out. The droplets from the oars sparkle in morning light. Against my skin my skirt is damp and cold. Kolya's familiar back bends with each stroke, so close I could reach out and touch it. Beside me, Vera clips her tangled blond hair into a barrette, arranges her pretty blue party dress which is spotted with wine, covered with twigs.

The docks and shacks slide past, then rowboats, tied to pilings, and the same brown horse staring over the fence. We are almost there. For me there will be an all-night train to Moscow, a plane to catch. Kolya will go to work without having slept, Alyosha return to his wife, Vera to her little daughter—all of us equally condemned to our lives. The fishermen will head in this evening, tomorrow set out again. Russia is a fish, slipped through my fingers.

Works Cited

Allende, Isabel, *Of Love and Shadows*

Anderson, Sherwood, *Winesburg, Ohio*

Babel, Isaac, "Crossing into Poland"

Baldwin, James, "Sonny's Blues"

Beard, Jo Ann, "The Fourth State of Matter"

Blew, Mary Clearman, "The Unwanted Child"

Bohjalian, Chris, *Water Witches*

Brown, Dan, *The Da Vinci Code*

Bryson, Bill, *A Walk in the Woods*, *In a Sunburned Country*

Carver, Raymond, "A Small, Good Thing," "Are These Actual Miles?"

Cheever, John ,"Artemis the Honest Well Digger," "The Golden Age"

Cisneros, Sandra, *The House on Mango Street*

Connell, Evan S., *Mr. Bridge*, *Mrs. Bridge*

Cooper, Bernard, "Burl's"

Crane, Stephen, "The Open Boat"

Cunningham, Michael, *A Home at the End of the World*

Dickens, Charles, *A Christmas Carol*, *A Tale of Two Cities*

Dillard, Annie, *Pilgrim at Tinker Creek*, "Living Like Weasels"

Doty, Mark, *Dog Years*

Ellison, Ralph, *Invisible Man*

Erdrich, Louise, *Love Medicine*, *The Blue Jay's Dance*, *Tracks*

Fielding, Helen, *Bridget Jones's Diary*

Fitzgerald, F. Scott, *The Great Gatsby*

Frucht, Abby, *Life Before Death*

Ghosh, Amitov, "The Ghosts of Mrs. Ghandi"

Haddon, Mark, *The Curious Incident of the Dog in the Night-Time*

Hall, Donald, "From Willow Temple"

Hemingway, Ernest, "The End of Something," *The Sun Also Rises*

Houston, Pam, "How to Talk to a Hunter"

Iyer, Pico, *Falling Off the Map: Some Lonely Places of the World*

Jones, Edward P., "The First Day"

Joyce, James, Ulysses, "The Boarding House"

Kincaid, Jamaica, *A Small Place*

Kingston, Maxine Hong, *The Woman Warrior*

Lahiri, Jumpa, "Unaccustomed Earth"

Lowry, Malcolm, *Under the Volcano*

Lynch, Thomas, *The Undertaking*

Márquez, Gabriel García, *One Hundred Years of Solitude*

McBride, James, *The Color of Water*

McCarthy, Cormac, *The Road*

Miller, Brenda, "The Date"

Mitchell, Margaret, *Gone With the Wind*

Moore, Lorrie, Anagrams, "People Like That are the Only People Here"

Morrison, Toni, *Song of Solomon*

Naylor, Gloria, *The Women of Brewster Place*

Oates, Joyce Carol, "Where Are You Going? Where Have Your Been?"

O'Brien, Tim, *The Things They Carried*

O'Connor, Flannery, "A Good Man Is Hard to Find"

Olmstead, Robert, "Cody's Story"

Orlean, Susan, "Show Dog"

Orwell, George, *Animal Farm*

Peery, Janet, "Whitewing"

Pullman, Philip, *The Golden Compass, The Amber Spyglass*

Redel, Victoria, *Loverboy*

Row, Jess, "The Secrets of Bats"

Schorer, Mark, "The Face Within the Face"

Schwartz, Delmore, "The World is a Wedding"

Sedaris, David, "Santaland Diaries," *Me Talk Pretty One Day*

Selzer, Richard, *Letters to a Young Doctor*

Silverman, Sue William, "The Pat Boone Fan Club"

Slater, Lauren, "Black Swans"

Sutin, Lawrence, *A Postcard Memoir*

Tallent, Elizabeth, "No One's a Mystery"

Tan, Amy, *The Joy Luck Club*

Thoreau, Henry David, *Walden*

Thubron, Colin, *Where Nights Are Longest, Shadow of the Silk Road*

Tolstoy, Leo, *Anna Karenina*

Twain, Mark, *The Adventures of Huckleberry Finn*

Updike, John, "The Persistence of Desire"

Wallace, David Foster, "Consider the Lobster"

Welty, Eudora "A Worn Path," "Why I Live at the P.O."

Wolff, Tobias, *In Pharoah's Army, This Boy's Life*

Yamanaka, Lois-Ann, *Blu's Hanging*

Index